# CRITICAL
# KNOWLEDGE
# TRANSFER

# CRITICAL KNOWLEDGE TRANSFER

## TOOLS FOR MANAGING YOUR COMPANY'S DEEP SMARTS

DOROTHY LEONARD ◆ WALTER SWAP ◆ GAVIN BARTON

HARVARD BUSINESS REVIEW PRESS

Boston, Massachusetts

Printed in the United States of America

10 9 8 7 6 5 4 3 2 1

The web addresses referenced in this book were live and correct at the time of the book's publication but may be subject to change.

Library of Congress Cataloging-in-Publication Data

Leonard-Barton, Dorothy.
    Critical knowledge transfer : tools for managing your company's deep smarts / Dorothy Leonard, Walter Swap, Gavin Barton.
        pages cm
    ISBN 978-1-4221-6811-0 (hardback)
    1. Knowledge management.   2. Mentoring in business.   3. Information resources management.   4. Information technology—Management.
    5. Technological innovations—Management.   I. Swap, Walter C.
    II. Barton, Gavin.   III. Title.
    HD30.2.L457  2014
    658.4'038—dc23                                                                    2014021493

The paper used in this publication meets the requirements of the American National Standard for Permanence of Paper for Publications and Documents in Libraries and Archives Z39.48-1992.

ISBN: 9781422168110
eISBN: 9781422168127

# Contents

Introduction     1

## PART ONE

## Laying the Foundations

1   The Problem: Losing Critical Knowledge     9

2   What Do You Need to Know about Knowledge?     17

3   Setting Up Knowledge Transfer: The Players Involved     43

## PART TWO

## Tools and Techniques

4   Smart Questioning     65

5   Capturing Deep Smarts—with Help     89

6   Accelerating the Transfer of Tacit Knowledge     117

7   Assessing the Transfer of Deep Smarts     143

8   The GE Global Research Centers Story     163

9   Socializing the Organization     181

*Notes*     *201*

*References*     *205*

*Index*     *209*

*Acknowledgments*     *215*

*About the Authors*     *217*

# Introduction

Do any of the following situations sound familiar?

1.  You've been hearing about the baby boomer retirements for years—but now the tsunami is upon you. The senior ranks of managers, scientists, and engineers are heading out for Sun City, and it is going to be challenging to fill the void. A lot of projects will be delayed or canceled for lack of seasoned employees. Of course, some of what is in their heads is obsolete. But how much? And what parts? What knowledge can and should be passed along to less experienced colleagues?

2.  You've been hiring talented young engineers and managers the past few years, but they're . . . different. They are very social, but prefer texting and tweeting to face-to-face meetings. And they really don't like to use telephones—even for sales! These Gen-Y folks, or millennials, are impatient to move up the organizational ladder and don't expect to spend twenty years in the same company. They have some great new ideas, such as using social media to interact with customers. But how do you integrate these ideas into the organizational culture?

3. You've just acquired a smaller company with some terrific new technical capabilities. The lawyers and accountants have been duly diligent for months now, but you are still not sure how much of the technology is really documented. How much will you have to rely on what's in the heads of the brilliant founders? What will be the value of the acquisition if they leave as soon as they are allowed to cash their retention bonuses and take their smarts with them?

4. Your product and service teams are scattered around the globe. It's great that someone in East Asia is working while your US team members are sleeping—and your electronic communication systems allow you to get really quick responses to a given specific problem. But how do you progress individuals and teams from competence to expertise, given that your experts are so dispersed?

All of these scenarios have a common challenge, and some common solutions. Whether you are a chief technology officer (CTO) overseeing a loss of experienced engineers; a chief information officer (CIO) who needs to keep software systems up and running regardless of departures; or a human resource director responsible for developing and retaining human capital, you will grapple with these questions: How can the business-critical, experience-based knowledge—what we call *deep smarts*—of a subject-matter expert or highly experienced manager possibly be transferred? When is it necessary or worthwhile? Will the transfer process take forever, or are there shortcuts?

Some readers already recognize the seriousness of the problem and are looking for solutions. But there are others who may be more skeptical. Perhaps you question the need for knowledge transfer; perhaps *expert* is linked in your mind with anti-innovation or old school. Some expertise should certainly not be targeted for transfer. That's why this book is about *critical* knowledge, not all knowledge. Moreover, it is about a particular subset of expertise—that which is experience based and still mostly undocumented, contained in the heads and hands of your employees.

While you have superb access to what you might call *know-what*, that is, facts, algorithms, well-documented processes, and the knowledge obtained through formal education or readily available on the web, so do your competitors. Such information is not as competitively valuable as the less imitable deep smarts in your organization—what the most valuable employees have learned to *do*—their *know-how*. That expertise includes such skills as the ability to diagnose and anticipate problems, relate to customers, make swift and wise judgment calls. Such know-how has a long shelf life and will be valuable well into the future; hence the need to transfer it to the next generation of managers and subject-matter experts.

You might wonder why, in this age of smartphones, driverless cars, and "big data," we choose to focus on the knowledge in peoples' heads, and on transferring that knowledge from one person to another, usually directly. We are certainly aware of the many benefits offered by technological advances: electronic tools that aid communication, computerized simulations that can provide a vicarious learning-by-doing experience, and increasingly sophisticated decision-support systems that can capture some expertise. But such systems rarely can stand alone—at best, they require a partnership with humans. Analysis of big data requires human judgment to see the patterns and develop plausible theories from statistical correlations. Eric Schadt, director of the Icahn Institute for Genomics and Multiscale Biology, comments on the need to present information and data "in a way that engages the human mind, which is a pretty amazing pattern recognition machine . . . Maybe 10, 20 years down the road, computers like [IBM's] Watson . . . are going to be good enough to where the human intervention is less. But today, that's not true."[1]

In one volume, we couldn't possibly cover all the myriad ways that software systems can complement the judgment of deeply smart people. Nor are such systems our own primary area of expertise.

You may have the opportunity to consider which deep smarts can be conveyed through such media and which are best left to human judgment. But in this book, we concentrate on the advantages of utilizing human "wetware." We therefore offer the reader insights and practical advice based on our deep grounding in human behavior and decades of experience with, and research on, knowledge transfer.

This book is written for the manager who suspects, or knows for certain, that vital knowledge is leaking out of the organization during job transitions of many kinds and who wishes to stanch the flow. The aim is to stop costly knowledge rework, without eliminating the potential for innovation.

We've organized the book into two parts (figure I-1), so that you may skim what might already be familiar and home in on our discussion of tools and techniques.

Part 1 provides the foundations for the rest of the book. Chapter 1 examines the costs of losing know-how. After all, if there is no reason for concern, why consider preserving knowledge? We report on what top executives we surveyed say their organizations are doing about those losses. In chapter 2, we focus on exactly what constitutes the business-critical and experience-based knowledge that is most valuable to your organization. You can't very well design

**FIGURE I-1**

**Road map of the book**

| Part 1: Foundations | Chapter 1: MOTIVATE (*WHY* transfer?) | Chapter 2: UNDERSTAND (Transfer *WHAT*?) | Chapter 3: PREPARE (*WHO* is involved?) | |
|---|---|---|---|---|
| Part 2: Tools and techniques | Chapters 4, 5, 6: SELECT (*WHICH* transfer options fit?) | Chapter 7: EVALUATE (*HOW* will we know it worked?) | Chapter 8: BENCHMARK (*WHAT* did GE do?) | Chapter 9: SOCIALIZE (*HOW* do we get buy-in?) |

transfer initiatives without a strong grasp of exactly what is to be transferred. The word *knowledge* covers too much territory. There are various types of knowledge, and they need to be transferred differently. Chapter 3 shows how to identify the critical knowledge and enlist the players who will be essential to any successful knowledge-transfer effort.

Part 2 covers the practical aspects of knowledge transfer. Chapters 4, 5, and 6 provide specific transfer options, with examples of tools and techniques. Some are appropriate for situations in which time is short, the need is critical, or resources are scarce. Under these circumstances, only the most easily accessible types of knowledge can be transferred. Other techniques are most effective when the organization has the luxury of time and can transfer more of the tacit, less accessible dimensions of deep smarts. Chapter 7 covers methods to assess the success of knowledge-transfer programs. In chapter 8, we bring you a tale from the trenches, with a detailed account of how GE's renowned Global Research Centers set up a knowledge-transfer program. And in chapter 9, we discuss how an organization can be socialized to accept knowledge-transfer initiatives, and we suggest ways to overcome common obstacles faced by managers in setting up such programs.

At the end of each chapter, we pose some questions designed to help you think about the issues that have been discussed and to create some action items for you or your staff. While most of these questions are directed at those of you who will be managing knowledge transfer, we also offer one or two questions for you to share with your team members to consider when they are knowledge-transfer recipients.

By the time you finish reading, you will have a comprehensive overview of knowledge transfer, including these important aspects of the process:

- The costs associated with knowledge loss

- The kinds of knowledge you need to preserve and pass along

- How to identify those valuable knowledge assets

- Proven tools and techniques being used by organizations
  to address both urgent and longer-term needs to transfer
  experience-based expertise—both technical and managerial

- The specific steps one organization went through to take on
  the challenge of preserving its world-class know-how

- How to socialize your organization, namely, how to persuade
  the people whose help you need that they too will benefit
  from a knowledge-transfer initiative

Human experts—managers as well as scientists and engineers—
are not obsolete yet! As long as we depend on experts' judgment, be
it their judgment alone or partnered with powerful decision support systems, all of us need to understand the importance of passing
knowledge on.

# PART ONE

# Laying the Foundations

BEFORE WE INTRODUCE you to the tools you might wish to use in transferring knowledge, we have to address some basic questions: Why would you spend resources on the transfer? What exactly do you need to transfer? And who must be involved? In our research and work in the field, we find that the answers to these questions can seem deceptively simple to managers. But these issues must be addressed with care before you will know which tools and techniques fit your particular situation. So let us turn to the first question: why transfer knowledge?

1

# The Problem:
# Losing Critical Knowledge

Does it really matter if we lose knowledge? That question can be answered a number of ways, including a consideration of your competitive environment and the potential effects of knowledge loss on corporate strategy. But let's start with the most immediate issue: how the loss of knowledge affects the bottom line.

## Invisible Hits to the Bottom Line

HR executives generally know the costs of recruiting, hiring, and training, whether incurred for freshly minted college graduates or for experienced knowledge workers. Of course, the costs still vary according to the industry, the size of the organization, its geographical dispersion, and its policies about hiring bonuses and relocation benefits; however, these are visible as line items in a budget. But such items weren't the only costs the director of human resources at Fort Wayne Metals had in mind when he declared, "Every time we hire someone, we are making a million-dollar decision."[1] He was talking about workers on the floor—not the occupants of the C-suite—and he was including all the intangible costs associated with integrating a new hire into the organization. These less easily quantifiable costs vary according to the number of years the workers have been in the industry and in the organization, the criticality of their expertise, and the extent of their professional networks. What is the cost of losing a key customer relationship? Of an extended project delay? How about a poor decision because of inexperience? Because these numbers are never found in budgets, are so hard to estimate, and may not show up immediately, they sometimes slip past those who might be the most negatively affected when the expert or experienced manager takes off to sail around the world.

Years ago, at the dawn of the quality movement, manufacturing organizations figured out that the costs of physical rework in factory operations were horrendous. Operators spent many hours a day correcting mistakes made on products produced upstream from them. Once recognized, the problem was relatively easy to quantify and rectify, compared with rework among knowledge workers today. Knowledge workers deal with products and services that are often intangible and even invisible. Rework is not obvious. Yet every transfer of responsibility during routine promotions, rotations, and relocation involves some loss and re-creation of knowledge as the incumbent is replaced by someone new to the job, and the loss is magnified when the new hire arrives from outside the organization. The new employees need to figure out more than the location of the restrooms and the cafeteria, and their initial reliance on team members for information slows everyone down. It's not all bad, of course. The new people may bring better skills, new perspectives, and creative ideas. But there's always some loss of productivity. Consider these examples from our recent research:

- The CTO at a *Fortune* 500 company inherited a research organization that hadn't produced any significant innovation in five years, despite using up $25 million designated for new-product development. The reason? A spate of firings and departures of key technical staff during the tenure of her predecessor. Projects were delayed, derailed, or canceled because of the lack of expertise.

- A financial services firm found that a thirty-year veteran in its regulatory division was leaving in a month. "Don't worry," he assured the company. "My direct reports know what I know." Sort of true. His direct reports do have a lot of experience themselves. But over the years, they've come to rely upon him for his ability to pick up the phone and get questions answered inside and outside the company from his huge network of contacts. They aren't sure how long it will be before they can step up to cover his work—if ever. Also, there is his encyclopedic memory of prior regulatory cases and his deep understanding of interactions among rules—knowledge that allowed him to make carefully reasoned decisions. They know he has kept them out of trouble for all those years, but not exactly how he has managed it, and they are worried that they won't know what they are missing until after he leaves.

- To figure out how much knowledge loss can potentially cost, the CIO at one *Fortune* 100 company looks at critical programs. "If a business is relying upon certain know-how and that is lost," he told us, "the resulting disruption could affect the entire business—perhaps twenty to thirty percent of a two-billion-dollar operation. And if the product itself is knowledge, and the company has to suspend operations, it could cost a hundred million."

- Jim Bethmann, managing partner at executive search firm Caldwell Partners, notes that there is an additional loss of productivity when a key person departs, because the survivors are hunkered down, operating "in neutral," not knowing whether they'll have a job in the future. "Everything suffers;

there is a change in momentum." Moreover, when a highly respected individual leaves a company, a cadre of colleagues often follow, taking with them additional critical know-how.[2]

It is very difficult, but not impossible, to put a price tag on losing key people and their deep smarts. When asked to estimate the costs associated with hiring new people (hiring bonuses, training, and head-hunting and relocation costs), most of the CIOs, CTOs, and HR executives we spoke to (see the sidebar "Survey of Top Executives" and figure 1-1) reported figures less than $50,000. But estimates of the *intangible* costs of losing key employees—lost professional networks, project delays, customer problems, and errors due to inexperience of the successor—were much higher, with 11 percent citing a figure greater than $1 million. As if to emphasize

## Survey of Top Executives

We contacted a number of CTOs, CIOs, and heads of HR departments in large (more than five hundred employees) US companies. Seventy-one of these top executives took the time to complete a brief survey on sharing critical, experience-based knowledge in their organizations. We also invited our respondents to engage in a short conversation with us to further discuss knowledge-transfer issues in their organizations. Fifteen took advantage of the offer, providing us with relevant tales from the field. The results of this survey, subsequent conversations with respondents, and interviews with several dozen additional executives and industry experts will be referred to at various points in this book. Some quotations from these conversations remain anonymous at the request of our respondents.

FIGURE 1-1

## Costs of losing key employees: estimated costs of hiring and less tangible costs per critical employee

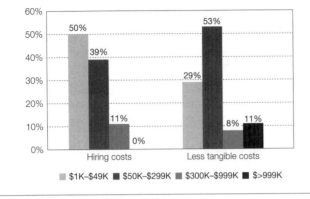

the intangible yet dire nature of these costs, some executives were unable to provide a dollar figure, but simply responded: "incalculable" or "priceless."

So even if you can't quantify the costs of knowledge loss to two decimal places, you might agree that the cost is often "a lot," enough that you would like some options to avoid or minimize those costs. Despite the acknowledged threat, a surprising number of our respondents reported that their organization was doing nothing or little about it (table 1-1).

## One More Cost: Loss of Capacity to Innovate

Innovation, especially in established companies, often emerges from new applications of deep smarts. For example, Grace Manufacturing was originally in the business of etching razor-sharp steel bands for computer printers. Realizing that the market was dying, company leaders asked themselves where the company's deep smarts resided. The answer was this: manufacturing sharp things. Management applied those patented skills first to a line of woodworking

TABLE 1-1

## Top responses of executives about their organizations' knowledge transfer

| Question (abbreviated) | Response |
|---|---|
| Does your organization need to transfer business-critical expertise? | 97% Yes<br>3% No |
| To what extent is your organization addressing that need? | 52% Not at all/somewhat<br>34% Quite a bit<br>14% A great deal |
| Is the threat of losing such expertise more or less of an issue than it was five years ago? | 78% More<br>22% About the same<br>0% Less |
| What are the most important situations requiring such transfer? (top four responses) | • Retirement of technical experts<br>• Younger generation's desire to move up<br>• Geographic dispersion<br>• Retirement of experienced managers |
| How frequently do you lose a top manager or another expert without a successor? | 16% Never<br>60% Sometimes<br>24% Frequently |
| In a specific, recent example of knowledge loss, was the individual's expertise managerial, technical, or both? | 59% Technical<br>10% Managerial<br>31% Both technical and managerial |
| What does your organization typically do about such losses? (top three responses) | • Exit interview<br>• Hire expert from outside organization<br>• Hire expert back as a consultant |

tools, then to a line of surgical instruments, and then to specialty cookware items such as graters, herb mills, and pizza cutters. Such culinary tools account for 65 percent of the company's income.[3]

Loss of proprietary know-how can actually cripple a company's ability to produce the next generation of products. Even radical innovations, with inventive leaps in performance, often call on organizational capabilities that have accrued over time. In 2004, when Boeing officially decided to build the Dreamliner 787 airplane, management anticipated that the aircraft would be the most revolutionary jetliner created in sixty years. The success of this enormously complicated project depended on the expertise held in the heads and hands of Boeing engineers, built up over years of working with the latest technologies and responding to complex customer requirements. However, with about half of the company's top technical staff eligible for retirement in the next several years, Boeing management realized that designing a disciplined process for gathering detailed insight, knowledge, and experience in developing airplanes was essential. As CTO John Tracy says, "You can't just write down how to create a new airplane and leave a page or two of instructions for the people after you. You need strategies and methods for capturing and sharing complex, unique, and hard-earned experience."[4]

Of course, no book can cover every way that companies capture or transfer critical knowledge, but we will share some prime examples of successful initiatives. Our research and work in the field have convinced us that there is value in providing an overview of knowledge-transfer experience—ours and that of others. Some of this you already know. But even veteran knowledge managers might gain some additional insights from our examples and anecdotes.

Take a look at the following questions to assess how much of a challenge knowledge loss is for you. If any of your answers indicate that you have a problem—or that your problem is bigger than you may have thought—then read on. We'll help you identify what kinds of knowledge you need to be thinking about. You can't—and shouldn't—transfer all knowledge. Just critical knowledge. That's the topic of our next chapter.

## Questions for Managers

1. How much of a problem is the loss of critical knowledge in your organization? Has the problem become more acute in recent years?

2. What kinds of situations requiring knowledge transfer are most important?

3.  Have there been incidents of mistakes, project delays, or problems with customers because a highly experienced employee left?

4.  How much do such departures cost?

5.  How does succession planning in your organization include knowledge-transfer processes?

## Questions for Knowledge Recipients

1.  Do you know of impending departures by people you rely on for advice, judgment calls, or other decisions?

2.  If so, can you suggest some knowledge-transfer efforts before they leave?

# 2

# What Do You Need to Know about Knowledge?

Before we explore *how* to transfer knowledge, we must understand *what* we propose to transfer. Not all knowledge is created equal; unless we are very sure of the differences, we can't design the transfer appropriately. This chapter introduces you to some nuances in the meaning of knowledge that will influence your selection of transfer tools and techniques.

## Data, Information, and Knowledge

Given the ubiquity of smartphones today, we might be forgiven for believing that opposable thumbs evolved to enable texting. That notion is somewhat less dangerous than a related one: that Siri or Google's search engine can deliver knowledge to the tips of our fingers. What those technologies provide are data and information—but not knowledge. Let us be clear. Data are discrete and "objective" facts, events, and numbers. Information is "data that makes a difference," that is, conveys some meaning.[1] In contrast, we define *knowledge* as:

> *Information that is relevant, actionable and at least*
> *partially based on experience.*[2]

Those three criteria (relevant, actionable, based on experience) help us find the chocolate chips in the cookie. Information that is not relevant to the purpose, carries no implications for action, and is entirely captured in written form—perhaps the description of a Doric column—can still be valuable, for sure. But for our purposes, that description is information, not knowledge, because it lacks the built-in experience factor. On the other hand, skillfully designing Doric columns into a building requires some experience-based skills—some real knowledge.

Part of the reason that Google transmits information and data rather than knowledge is that *experience* differentiates individuals who have the same access to information, perhaps also the same formal education. Relatively little of an individual's daily life experience is captured in some form that can be uploaded to a computer—especially experience that inspires knowledge. Granted, individuals who tweet every bit and byte of their lives to their followers leave behind a thick trail of documentation, and we can sometimes learn something useful within those 140 characters. Nevertheless, knowledge is more than an aphorism, a haiku, a proverb. The kinds of experience that build skills are those that have meaning beyond the moment and from which we actively learn. And knowledge exists at different levels of accessibility—hence the need to understand those levels in order to plan for transfer.

## Explicit, Implicit, and Tacit Knowledge

Let us introduce you to a deeply smart scientist ("Dr. S"). He has more than two hundred patents to his name, and his expertise about air flows places him in the absolute top ranks of that knowledge domain internationally. But if you picture him as a wizened, elderly fellow with Coke-bottle glasses who hides in a laboratory, you are way off track. A vigorous, charming extrovert who speaks several languages (besides differential equations), Dr. S has lived and worked in several countries. He has enormous depths of knowledge and an extensive professional network composed of experts from wide-ranging fields. He is very articulate in explaining air flows, whether to peers or ignorant visitors. Perhaps even more important, he likes to do so. He's an ideal source to transfer all kinds of knowledge, at different levels of accessibility. Figure 2-1 summarizes the types of knowledge and the resultant different levels of accessibility.

## *Explicit Knowledge*

Some of Dr. S's knowledge is like nuggets of gold right on the surface of the ground. This knowledge is explicit; that is, it comes in text, algorithmic, or pictorial form and is therefore relatively easy to transfer. His bookshelf contains hard copies of scientific texts to which he refers. Bookmarks on his computer indicate websites he finds useful. And his electronic files of papers, abstracts, presentations, reports,

FIGURE 2-1

### Accessing explicit, implicit, and tacit knowledge

| | | |
|---|---|---|
| Easier to access | *Explicit:* | Documented in some textual, visual, or auditory form; can be provided by the expert without much, if any, additional verbal explanation |
| | *Implicit:* | |
| | 1 | Not formally documented, but can be mapped as categories of tasks, skills, or roles |
| | 2 | Not documented or embedded in processes but can be articulated by the expert in rules, steps, stages, or techniques |
| More difficult to access | *Tacit:* | |
| | 1 | Never articulated before, but can be explained by experts through smart questioning |
| | 2 | Not recognized as knowledge by expert (knowledge is often unconscious) |

his list of contacts—all of these—are valuable contributors to his knowledge base. Give his team member a big enough flash drive to download it all, and presto, instant knowledge base. But of course it isn't quite that easy. Helpful, yes, definitely. But unless Dr. S goes through all these sources with his team members in some detail, these nuggets provide footprints rather than paths to knowledge. You can see where he has been, but not much about what is really critical, how he used it, and how it connects with his experience. The challenge for any successor would be to create real meaning from these fragments.

## Implicit Knowledge

Because all knowledge is linked with experience, much of it may lie dormant until a situation fires up the requisite neurons and the individual reacts swiftly and expertly. Inside Dr. S's head is a lot of knowledge that he has never been called on to record for posterity, or even to articulate. This realm of the *as yet* unarticulated and unwritten we call *implicit knowledge*. The as-yet distinction is important, because much of this kind of knowledge can be made explicit through some relatively painless processes of smart questioning.

### Level 1 Implicit Knowledge: Undocumented but Easily Articulated

If people really want to emulate at least a portion of the expertise that makes Dr. S so valuable to his organization, they will have to dig into its implicit dimensions. Level 1 implicit knowledge refers to knowledge that is in Dr. S's head, but can be fairly easily accessed. He has never written down all the tasks and responsibilities that occupy his day—but he can tell you *what he does* and *what he believes his skills are*. Notice we said "what he believes." An expert doesn't always know what others perceive to be the expert's best skills and capabilities. In fact, an expert may overestimate one capability ("I'm a great teacher") and underestimate another ("I build lots of prototypes—but so does every scientist"). There are a number of ways to access this top-of-the-mind, unarticulated knowledge, including the knowledge-elicitation tools discussed in chapters 4 and 5.

### Level 2 Implicit Knowledge: Rule-Based

Level 2 implicit knowledge is a bit less obvious and embodies more experience. The experts have organized their diagnostics and thought processes into coherent steps or have developed rules of thumb that can be shared. A US Secret Service official once explained that a rule he gave new agents assigned to crowd control for a VIP was, "Don't pay attention to the noisy people. Look for the quiet ones—they are more likely to be the threat." The newbies still have to figure out for themselves when such rules apply—but at least the articulation conveys some experience-based wisdom. Similarly, our deeply smart Dr. S suggested a rule of thumb to his probable successor: "Never try just one solution to a technical problem. Pursue a number in parallel. Some of my best inventions have been compiled from different pieces of various problem-solving approaches."

## *Tacit Knowledge*

Tacit knowledge is what we know—but often can't articulate—at least not immediately, and often never. This knowledge is subconscious. When we hear people say that they made a good decision based on gut feel, we can be reasonably sure there is tacit knowledge involved. Some of Dr. S's success is probably due to unconscious and unexamined smarts. His team members mentioned his ability to look at a prototype piece of research equipment and intuit whether it would be too expensive to construct. They were also in awe of how he communicated with clients, for example, explaining a disappointing research result so adroitly that the clients were convinced to fund further studies. How did he infer the best approach and adjust on the fly by reading their responses to what he was saying?

## Level 1 Tacit Knowledge: Understood but Can't Be Articulated

These skills of Dr. S are examples of level 1 *tacit* knowledge—when experts know that they are performing a difficult feat, but can't always explain what they thought and why they decided as they did.

A famous example of level 1 tacit knowledge skills is chicken sexing—determining if a newly hatched chick is male or female. As it turns out, this is a life-or-death decision for the chicken. Females are more highly valued for their reproductive ability, males for their meat. The Zen-Nippon Chick Sexing School in Japan taught people how to do this, and a novice had to go through as many as two years of training before being able to make the distinction in seconds. There are thousands of configurations involving certain arrangements of lines in a pullet, and male equipment the size of a pinhead in a cockerel. Apprentices learned to make the critical distinctions by trial and error, with a master standing by to judge if the chick had been tossed in the correct bin. But neither master nor apprentice could articulate the differences that guided their decisions.

During World War II, the British employed a similar method to transfer the ability of certain experts who could quickly distinguish British planes returning home from German planes coming to bomb, partly by engine sounds. The experts were totally unable to explain their methods of diagnosis. They could train others only by having the novice guess—and then having the expert agree or disagree. Eventually the novices absorbed the ability themselves, but—like the experts—the trainees were unable to state *how* they made their decisions.[3]

In both these examples, the ability to make fine, accurate distinctions among different visual or auditory cues was so difficult to articulate that the only way to transfer that know-how was to build it into a learner's consciousness through experience. As we will show in chapter 6, this mode of transfer can be emulated for business purposes—and accelerated through some specific techniques.

### Level 2 Tacit Knowledge: Unconscious

Some behaviors and thinking processes are so deeply buried that even their practitioners are totally unaware of them. The expert chicken-sexers and plane spotters were conscious of their behavior; they just couldn't explain it. But experts also display their deep smarts in ways that only other people can observe. Body language and speech patterns, for example, are often unconscious, and yet very important in communication. What makes one speaker engaging and another not, when both speakers are talking about the same topic and maybe with the same material? (See the sidebar "A Thin Slice of Expertise" for an example of how a "thin slice" of mere speech patterns can distinguish high-performing sales managers from more ordinary ones.) What does a conductor do that provokes the very best from an orchestra? Italian maestro Carlo Maria Giulini says his art is "very mysterious . . . I have no idea what I do up there."[4] A careful observer might notice that he uses his left hand differently than some conductors, or that his eye contact is particularly intense—but it might take an expert to even perceive such subtleties.

## *Tacit Knowledge and the Mind's Eye*

To complicate transfer even more, we store some knowledge as visual images. In fact, as Steven Pinker's work has shown, the phrase *mind's eye* is not just metaphorical. The same part of the brain lights up (albeit not as intensely) when people are invited to *think about* faces as when they *see* the faces. The same is true for places: the brain lights up similarly when people think about places as when they see them.[5]

Experts often use visual cues along with scientific processes to diagnose problems or make predictions. Medical professionals do this all the time, of course—but so do other experts. The managing director of a South African coal company says, "I only hire old

# A Thin Slice of Expertise

*Thin-slice research*, which describes the surprising tendency of people to make sweeping and enduring judgments based on very limited observation, has been replicated in many situations. For example, students' inferences about the personality characteristics of teachers based on a thirty-second videotape accurately predicted end-of-semester student course evaluations. In another study, undergraduates listened to sixty-second audio clips randomly extracted from interviews with twelve regional sales managers, half of whom had been designated as average and half as outstanding, according to ratings by supervisors and by actual sales effectiveness. The tapes were filtered to remove content, but preserved normal inflections and speech rhythms. After listening to the tapes, the subjects rated each manager on a series of scales, including several measuring interpersonal traits such as "enthusiastic" and "empathic." The sales managers whom the students rated more positively were much more likely to be those judged by their supervisors as outstanding. The results were virtually identical in a second study in which the tapes were not filtered, allowing the listeners to hear the content of the thin slices of interviews.[a]

a. Nalini Ambady, Mary Anne Krabbenhoft, and Daniel Hogan, "The 30-Sec Sale: Using Thin-Slice Judgments to Evaluate Sales Effectiveness," *Journal of Consumer Psychology* 16, no. 1 (2006): 4–13.

geologists." Why? Because they can look for visual cues as well as instrument-derived ones. Anthills over three feet high, for example, yield samples dug up by the obliging insects from some three to four meters below the surface. And those samples can be visually scanned for flecks of gold and other metals and for fossils that predate coal formations. If geologists see such fossils, they know that no coal lies below the surface, as it would have covered up the fossils. Despite all the new tools—GPS, radar, 3-D software—oldsters seem to be better at finding the patterns in the rocks than their younger colleagues. For example, rock cores drilled from the earth every few meters provide only sporadic information. "Age and experience help your imagination paint a picture of what's in between," explains Scott McLean, CEO of Transitions Metals Corp.[6]

## Deep Smarts: All Three Kinds of Knowledge

As the example of Dr. S suggests, deeply smart individuals have all three kinds of knowledge: they have explicit knowledge from formal education and embedded in manuals, websites, memos, and corporate documents. But their implicit and tacit knowledge, based on their experience, is the source of their greatest value. In researching this book, we've encountered many other deeply smart people with different kinds of expertise. For example, we recall a subject-matter expert with twenty-five years of experience in the company who is lightning fast with a diagnosis and almost always spot-on. Then, there is the product development manager whose team everyone wants to be on because he's so good at motivating and mentoring. And the vice president of sales with a terrific record of closing deals and leaving his clients smiling.

Interestingly, across all sorts of knowledge domains and types of expertise, such individuals have certain predictable characteristics or indicators. Not all deeply smart people exemplify all of them. Often, one or two skills don't fit neatly into the lists of characteristics,

TABLE 2-1

## What are the indicators of deep smarts?[a]

| Dimension | Deep smarts depend on |
|---|---|
| **Cognitive** | |
| Critical know-how and "know-what" | Managerial, technical, or both; superior, experience-based techniques and processes; extraordinary factual knowledge |
| System thinking | Knowing interdependencies, anticipating consequences, understanding interactions |
| Judgment | Rapid, wise decision making |
| Context awareness | Ability to take context into account |
| Pattern recognition | Swift recognition of a phenomenon, situation, or process that has been encountered before |
| **Behavioral** | |
| "Know-who" (networking) | Building and maintaining an extensive network of professionally important individuals |
| Interpersonal | Ability to deal with individuals, including motivating and leading them; comfort with intellectual disagreement |
| Communication | Ability to construct, tailor, and deliver messages through one or more media to build logical and persuasive arguments |
| Diagnosis and cue seeking | Ability to actively identify cues in a situation that would confirm or challenge a familiar pattern; ability to distinguish signal from noise |
| **Physical** | |
| Sensory intelligence | Ability to diagnose, interpret, or predict through touch or other sensory modalities |

a. These indicators have been somewhat revised from those enumerated in Dorothy Leonard and Walter Swap, *Deep Smarts: How to Cultivate and Transfer Enduring Business Wisdom* (Boston: Harvard Business School Press, 2005), in light of subsequent research. The major differences are the addition of three more behavioral indicators and the physical dimension.

but are particular to that job or that individual. Table 2-1 lists the indicators of deep smarts—cognitive, behavioral, and, occasionally, physical—that we most reliably see in highly valued employees.

This set of indicators helps to identify people with deep smarts, to explain and communicate the nature of deep smarts, and to measure the progress of individuals who are working to assimilate those smarts from people who have them. Skipping over the first characteristic for the moment (we'll see lots of examples throughout the book), let's consider in more depth the rest.

## System Perspective (Organizational and Technical)

Deeply smart individuals have a grasp of the whole system relevant to their role, including the ability to anticipate interactions and foresee the unintended consequences of decisions on other parts of the system. Two kinds of systems are particularly relevant to knowledge transfer: the way the organization works (which invariably involves another characteristic of deep smarts—networking) and the interactions of component parts in products, processes, or services.

To take the first: when new hires enter an organization, whether at entry level or in the C-suite, they need to understand the culture and history of how things are done, even—perhaps especially—if they intend to subsequently alter the system. What kinds of knowledge are revered, and what kinds disparaged? Who wields influence? How do departments interact? How do you get projects approved? Whom can you approach for credible answers?

A chief marketing officer in one of the companies clustered around Washington, D.C. (referred to—affectionately if you work at them—as the "Beltway Bandits") was known for his knowledge of the government contracting system. He had government contacts who informed him of pending legislation that could affect his business, and he was renowned for his ability both to foresee the implications of the legislation and to influence its shape by judicious lobbying. He knew whom and what to address. His selection of targets depended on his understanding of *two* systems—his own organization's and that of Congress. When he decided to go through the revolving door into government service (again), the company sought in vain for a replacement with comparable smarts.

The second kind of system knowledge is technical for engineers, financial for accountants, customer for marketing personnel, talent management for HR—and for the C-suite, it's usually a mixture of these. As we will see in illustrations of this kind of systemic knowledge, individuals with deep smarts can predict interactions among subsystems, see the implications of decisions and actions that are beyond the scope of less experienced employees, and understand the big picture. This ability enables these experts to avoid mistakes to which individuals with a more circumscribed viewpoint are vulnerable.

## Judgment and Context Awareness

Experts of all kinds can adapt their recommendations and actions to a variety of situations. Expert marketers know how to address various customer segments; market traders can distinguish among subtly different kinds of derivatives or swaps; rocket scientists know how to separate out data on normal wind turbulence from the internally generated "flutter" of a rocket. And they all make judgment calls based on fine distinctions that are invisible to less experienced individuals. These abilities make the experts especially valuable.

Here, a wild-land fire expert explains how he uses his understanding of the local flora to manage burning that has been prescribed to control the undergrowth in specified areas:

> One of the problems we have with different fuel types inside of a
> burn block is, for instance, young pine plantations . . . Longleaf is
> just one of the pines that . . . we have to be concerned about when
> it's in the plantation or the young stage . . . And loblolly and slash,
> two other pines . . . they can take fire, but not near as hot a fire . . .
> as longleaf . . . If you send a fire through longleaf when it's in the
> grass stage or from a year to two or three years old, it probably won't
> hurt it at all, no matter what kind of fire it is. But if it's . . . slash
> and loblolly, if you send any kind of fire through there when it's one
> to five years old, you're probably going to kill it all. So that's one of
> the areas that you're going to have to burn a little different . . .
> You can actually run a twenty-foot head fire across there, and it

*won't kill them . . . If the longleaf is four to six foot high, then you don't want four- to six-foot flame length because . . . it'll kill that size tree. It'll cook the cambium layer and also get the bud too . . . So what you try to do is to figure out what type fire you need there, and that's the way you burn. You know, if it's six-foot trees, then you can backfire . . . If they're in the grass stage, then you need to run the fire across them at a faster rate.*[7]

Of some frustration to such wild-land fire experts was the inability of relatively new hires to make such nuanced decisions. None of the available computer models enables inexperienced new hires to decide what kind of fire should be matched to the kind of flora in the area to be burned over.

## Pattern Recognition

Pattern recognition essentially underlies almost all the other characteristics—including physical. It is born of experience. What is often termed *intuition* is really very swift pattern recognition. It occurs so quickly that the individuals don't realize they have sorted through experiences with prior situations and a host of considerations before "intuiting" a decision. Consider the following case.

A fifty-four-year old woman came to the emergency room with a saucer-sized, suppurating ulcer on her calf. The ER doctor diagnosed an infection and began intravenous antibiotics. However, by the third day, there was no improvement, and Nadine Stanojevic, an internal medicine resident, remembered from her internship days a patient who had a similar ulcer. The earlier patient did not have an infection, but instead suffered from pyoderma gangrenosum, a rare skin disorder particularly difficult to diagnose because it so closely resembles the more common bacterial infections. Stanojevic mentioned this possibility to the attending physician, Jeremy Schwartz, who had never seen a case of pyoderma gangrenosum, and the attending doctor continued to think it was an infection.

However, when a culture failed to grow bacteria, Stanojevic again mentioned the skin disorder, this time explaining that she had seen a case of pyoderma gangrenosum before. Given the new, correct diagnosis, the medical staff administered steroids and the patient quickly recovered.

Schwartz later told a reporter, "She'd seen a case, and I'd never seen one. I felt like she was more of an authority than I was . . . [Pyoderma gangrenosum] is one of these things with long Latin names that you read about but you don't really know it until you see it. Once you see it, though, you'll never miss it." Note that in this case, it was the *junior* physician who assumed the role of expert and convinced her superior of the validity of her diagnosis, because she *had* seen it before. Her experience—rare as it was—allowed her to identify a pattern her colleague had never seen.[8]

## *"Know-Who" (Networking)*

Maybe you know someone like "Purnima." After twenty-six years in the organization and working with federal agencies, she can pick up the phone and reach anyone she needs. But Purnima is leaving her position unexpectedly, and she hasn't had time to introduce her junior colleagues to their new boss, take them to meetings, or bring them in on conference calls. So she hasn't transferred any of her social capital. A junior colleague was frustrated when Purnima pointed out that he could get to information sources the same way that she could—going through the heads of corporate departments. "But," he protested, "you can go right to the top, talk to the CEO. And he will answer your call. I can't do that."

Deeply smart people—experienced executives and subject-matter experts alike—live in a web of relationships built up over years. They can easily pass along the explicit contact information of email and snail mail addresses and phone numbers. As a remarkable scientist once observed, "Smart people know [other] smart people."[9] Their networks are not just a list of LinkedIn connections; they know *which* person to call for what kinds of information. Say they need to know how to use social media in marketing. If they don't know how themselves, they may know someone who fills the bill. At worst, they can get online or on the phone to a colleague and be directed to another contact who knows such an expert. This is valuable social capital, based on years of reciprocal help. So how can you transfer *that*? You can't entirely, of course, but as we will discuss further in part 2, the expert or executive can introduce a successor and jump-start the relationship building.

## Interpersonal Skills

Ever have a boss for whom you felt an intense personal loyalty? We met such a manager in a highly technical organization. Rebecca's team members said they wanted to "go the extra mile for her" and to "deliver for her." They described "working for the project and team rather than for a paycheck." They talked about their work for her as a personal relationship that involves "caring" and the sense of a "family." Mind you, they also talked about high standards; this leader is highly valued by her organization for her performance—not her ability to motivate her team. Yet the latter surely leads to the former. Later in the book, we will see just how she inspires this kind of motivation. There are many types of interpersonal skills, most of them related to emotional intelligence. For Rebecca, they include not only her ability to manage her team well, but also her talent for collaboration, cooperation, wise hiring and firing, cultural sensitivity, and many others.

## Communication

Rarely does someone who is highly valued for critical, experience-based business knowledge not also excel at some form of communication—and it is not always oral. Some people have the ability to write concise, persuasive reports and other documents.

Others excel at representing complex processes in schematic form. A few individuals may combine two or all three forms of communication. Not surprisingly, Rebecca, the manager profiled earlier, is also an excellent communicator. She is often selected by her managers to take visiting dignitaries and the press on tours of the facilities, because she is so articulate. Her team finds her ability to communicate with clients amazing. She seems to know exactly how to present data so that it becomes a compelling and very clear story.

## Diagnosis and Cue Seeking

Gurpreet Dhaliwal, an associate professor of clinical medicine at the University of California, San Francisco, is revered for his ability to diagnose extremely difficult cases. At a recent medical convention, he was given an ambiguous case to diagnose in forty-five minutes— on stage, in front of six hundred peers! Journalist Katie Hafner describes how the doctor applies his talents:

> To observe him at work is like watching Steven Spielberg tackle a script or Rory McIlroy a golf course. He was given new information bit by bit—lab, imaging, and biopsy results. Over the course of the session, he drew on an encyclopedic familiarity with thousands of syndromes. He deftly dismissed red herrings while picking up on clues that others might ignore, gradually homing in on the accurate diagnosis . . . At work he occasionally uses a diagnostic checklist program called Isabel, just to make certain he hasn't forgotten something. But the program has yet to offer a diagnosis that Dr. Dhaliwal missed.[10]

His ability illustrates what expert human brains are capable of—pattern recognition and separating out the true signal from the noise. However, programs like Isabel are helpful because, as its creator points out, "low-frequency events are hard to put on the brain's palette . . . It's impossible for any one person to remember how each of those diseases presents, because each presents with a different pattern."[11] Another program, IBM's Watson for Healthcare, is very good at accessing and analyzing in mere seconds huge masses of text, including patient records, textbooks, and journal articles—material that the physician could hardly have had time in an entire career to absorb. The program is learning to interpret clinical information, but it has yet to focus directly on diagnosis. What computer systems still find difficult is working with incomplete or imprecise information—as diagnosticians must.

Deeply smart individuals are particularly adept at not only recognizing patterns but also hypothesizing possible patterns by running through a set of individual diagnostics—what we call *cue seeking*. On a trip through a factory in the company of a vice president of manufacturing, one of us was surprised to see him bending over to scrutinize the underside of the conveyor belts. Why was he doing that? "Because if the bearings are rusty," he answered, "that's an indicator that maintenance is likely a problem in this facility. Next I'll check out the men's room and see if the faucets are tight or leaky." He was seeking cues that would suggest a pattern: slovenly versus careful maintenance.

## Sensory Intelligence

Skills are embodied not only in our minds but also in our bodies. Consider three very diverse examples of embodied skills, all of which are built through years of experience and exhaustive (and exhausting) practice: athletes, sleight-of-hand magicians, and engineers who are producing physical products. Professional athletes practice moves until the mechanics are ingrained in motor memory. When all-star National Basketball Association guard Steve Nash was asked what he does better now that he's thirty-eight (!), he replied: "Reading situations is more second nature. Different moments of the game slow down a little bit."[12] He's noticing things,

# Embodied Tactile Knowledge

In his book *Fooling Houdini*, Alex Stone visits a number of presti-digitators to learn the tricks of their professions, but none was as remarkable as Richard Turner. At a lecture for the Society of American Magicians, Turner performed several astonishing card tricks, including these:

- Demonstrating repeated, rapid-fire cutting and shuffling of a deck (sometimes with one hand) in front of an audience volunteer, announcing that the deck should now be well shuffled, then spreading the deck face up to show the cards in perfect numerical order

- Dealing blackjacks (two cards totaling 21) to another volunteer every time, after she had shuffled and cut the deck

- And, most baffling of all to the room filled with professional magicians, asking a spectator to select a card, replace it in the deck, and shuffle the deck, only to have Turner bring the card to the top of the deck

Oh, and one more thing. Richard Turner is blind.

After many years of practice (including literally sleeping with his cards) and aided perhaps by a compensatory response to his degenerative eye disease, Turner achieved "an almost superhuman tactile ability."[a] He consults to casinos and to the United States Playing Card Company, with the job title *touch analyst*.

a. Alex Stone, "The Touch Analyst," chap. 4 in *Fooling Houdini: Magicians, Mentalists, Math Geeks, and the Hidden Powers of the Mind* (New York: HarperCollins, 2012).

making instant decisions from his observation, built over years of experience.

Deep smarts based on tactile intelligence can be found in unexpected places. See the sidebar "Embodied Tactile Knowledge" for an example of tactile "magic."

The deep smarts embodied in the hands of a physician, a technician, or an engineer can be just as impressive as those of athletes and magicians. The expertise of engineers is perhaps most relevant to this book, given that many of the deeply smart individuals whose knowledge is at risk of being lost are scientists and engineers. In fact, some would argue that basic manual skills that youths used to accumulate by building go-carts or helping with home improvement projects have largely bypassed the generation growing up now. (See the sidebar "Boeing's Opportunities for New Engineers Program" for an example of how one large engineering company is dealing with this paucity of hands-on skills.) Newly graduated

## Boeing's Opportunities for New Engineers Program

One of the challenges facing manufacturers that create physical products requiring a blend of high-tech electronics and physical components is the limited experience today's young people have working with physical objects. As one of us (Dorothy) and Tim Bridges, director of knowledge management for Boeing, note in an HBR blog, few Americans grow up tinkering with cars.[a] Instead, eight- to eighteen-year-olds spend fifty-three hours a week with entertainment media.

For Boeing, the resulting lack of tactile intelligence is a serious issue: "Many have no practiced knowledge about how metal or plastic bends, breaks, retains heat or burns, no practical understanding of how to limit size for fuel efficiency while allowing enough space for technicians to reach inside and connect components. If you haven't physically handled and experimented with woods, metals, plastics, it's difficult to imagine how to engineer an airplane wing that can, for example, keep bending to 140 percent of its maximum load without damage, and only fail beyond that."

Boeing has decided to close this knowledge gap through its Opportunities for New Engineers program. Recent hires work with senior engineer mentors in projects ranging from building a miniature airplane from the design stage through flying, to working in a thirty-two-person team to "build, certify, and fly" a Glasair Super II airplane. The finished products must meet stringent requirements. The mentored employees "see and feel how the parts physically fit or don't. They understand the touch and finesse needed to bend the wing and the physical strength of a thick versus a thin cross section. They see where years of engineering theory clash with harsh realities."

a. Dorothy Leonard and Tim Bridges, "Why Kids—and Workers—Need to Get Their Hands Dirty," *HBR Blog Network*, October 9, 2013, http://blogs.hbr .org/2013/10/why-kids-and-workers-need-to-get-their-hands-dirty/.

engineers know their physics, but they may have no sense of what a vibration, unexpected heat, or tool "chatter" might signify. Manufacturing companies complain that they can't find the workers they need. Fort Wayne Metals, for example, struggles with this scarcity of tactile skills and has a hard time finding workers with the adequate skills for the factory floor.[13]

# Personality-Based Skills

Some skills can't be transferred, because they are based on personality rather than experience or practice. We are born with some preferences, as simultaneously generic and individual as fingerprints. They shape the skills we develop.

For example, "Harry" sees life as a mosaic. He loves detail; you can't give him too much. He is valued in his company for his ability to patiently and systematically assemble the pieces of a corporate puzzle and then present the whole as a coherent recommendation based on intricately interconnected bits of evidence. He describes himself, self-deprecatingly (but not clinically), as obsessive-compulsive, as a way of explaining his passion for the nitty-gritty. His colleagues sometimes find him irritatingly immersed in their own areas of expertise because he wants to understand *everything*. When he leaves his position, others could take up the slack, but the danger is that in their intensely risky business, some tiny overlooked pebble could cause an avalanche, one that Harry routinely anticipates. No one else has quite his appetite for detail.

Such personal talents are unlikely to be replicated when the individual possessing them moves on. So we concentrate only on the skills that can be taught. But those are quite enough to be valuable.

# Where Deep Smarts Come From

Where did you get your own deep smarts, particularly your ability to detect patterns in a complex array of information or anticipate interactions in a system you operate? We would be surprised if you didn't say it came from your experience.

K. Anders Ericsson and his colleagues have argued that there are two essential ingredients in attaining true expertise.[14] First, you must engage in concentrated effort, often involving sacrifice and struggle—what they term "deliberate practice." Second, a budding expert needs a skilled coach or mentor to guide the practice, to correct errors and reinforce progress. While perhaps demonstrated most clearly in our earlier discussion of physical and sensory intelligence of athletes and magicians, deliberate practice with expert feedback is necessary for the development of any kind of expertise. (We will explore this topic more in chapter 6, where we discuss how you might structure practice most efficiently and effectively.)

In research at a large software company that we will describe at greater depth in chapter 3, we designed a study to test the ability of deep-smarts indicators to distinguish between participants who were considered deeply smart and those who were satisfactory and competent—but not superstars. Even though the pairs of employees were quite evenly matched on experience, we found sufficient variation to develop an objective overall experience index (age, years since graduating from college, years in the industry, years at the company). We learned that even minor variations in experience can make a big difference: employees who scored highest on the experience index were also rated significantly higher in deep smarts by both their direct managers and their coworkers. These were the employees that the company was especially eager to retain and whose knowledge was most valuable.

Experience alone, of course, is rarely sufficient to develop deep smarts. We all know individuals whose skills, for various reasons—personality factors, motivation, genetic endowment—stopped developing at a level of adequacy or competence. For others, mere repetition of well-learned tasks may have locked in old, perhaps maladaptive, habits. The manager who has run hundreds of meetings and who therefore could have developed some communication and interpersonal smarts, may have instead honed some nasty habits—ignoring or dismissing dissent or cutting people off—that have never been pointed out to him or her by the cowed audience. (This is why feedback from a trusted—and knowledgeable—mentor can be an essential addition to experience.)

# The Limits of Experience-Based Knowledge

In some cases, however, experience is not a good guide, either because the environment is inherently volatile and unpredictable or because the situation is totally unprecedented. In such cases, we caution against relying on and transferring expert judgments, because there are no reliable patterns to recognize. Two widely respected thinkers provide some insight into when to trust the intuition of experts—and hence, when their knowledge should be targeted for transfer.

Gary Klein, whose research has been based largely on such experts as firefighters and chess grand masters, emphasizes the importance of experience: "What enables us to make good decisions is intuition, in the form of very large repertoires of patterns acquired over years and years of practice."[15] Nobel Prize winner Daniel Kahneman is skeptical of the intuitive leaps of many experts, no matter what their experience, because of the many well-documented biases that shape our perceptions and our behaviors. These two scholars resolved their debate, at least in part, by considering the different domains in which intuition is exercised. An accumulation of experiences enables the expert firefighter and chess player to learn patterns that may be recognized so rapidly that their "intuitive" recognition seems—at least in the absence of skillful probing—inexplicable. On the other hand, Kahneman argues, when a task is inherently unpredictable or chaotic, no amount of experience will enable the expert's intuitions to rise above base rates: "Stock-pickers and political scientists who make long-term forecasts operate in a zero-validity environment. Their failures reflect the basic unpredictability of the events that they try to forecast."[16]

So if a system is made up of random elements, then expertise is impossible. Any choice will be, well, random, and an expert's guidance may be no better than that of a novice. There are no expert roulette players.

# The Best Stock Pickers: "Experts," Indexes, or Monkeys?

Inspired by economist Burton Malkiel's assertion that stock-picking pros would not outperform a blindfolded monkey throwing darts at the financial pages, the *Wall Street Journal* initiated its famous Dartboard Contest in 1988. *WSJ* staffers, standing in for their biological cousins, dutifully threw darts, and investment pros picked theirs. The results were then compared after six months. Over the next ten years, the experiment was repeated one hundred times, and the "monkeys," the experts, and the Dow Jones Industrial Average (DJIA) were compared. Take heart (at least a little) if you rely on the advice of a stock professional: the pros beat the monkeys 61 percent of the time. However, the pros beat the DJIA only 51 percent of the time. Furthermore, the monkeys' picks continued to do well after six months, whereas the pros' picks fell.[a]

a. Jason Unger, "Can Monkeys Pick Stocks Better than Experts?" accessed May 20, 2014, www.automaticfinances.com/monkey-stock-picking/.

Stock markets are, according to many economists, efficient. That is, an investor cannot, over time, achieve returns beyond market averages, given available information. According to these economists, it is a fool's errand to hand over money to an "expert" stock analyst, rather than putting one's money into index funds. (See the sidebar "The Best Stock Pickers: 'Experts,' Indexes, or Monkeys?" for a test of this controversial conclusion.)

Similarly, when events or situations are totally *unprecedented*, there is no experience on which to build a repertoire of possible outcomes—no known patterns. For example, recent forest fires in the western United States have been so large and volatile that one fire "wasn't carried by embers, but marched inexplicably over snow. No one had seen that before."[17] Expert experience was no help to the firefighters. Nassim Taleb coined the term "black swans" to represent large, unexpected events with important consequences: "We never see black swans coming, but when they do arrive, they profoundly shape our world: Think of World War I, 9/11, the Internet, the rise of Google."[18] In such situations, experts cannot call on recognizable patterns. Rather, deeply smart individuals know what they don't know; in the absence of recognizable patterns, they must apply their critical thinking, system awareness, and diagnostic abilities.

So identifying individuals whose knowledge needs to be transferred is not as simple as noting those with the most experience. In chapter 3, we will describe a few ways that organizations can identify experts (including experienced managers) to emulate.

## Questions for Managers

1. How could you help your employees and colleagues distinguish knowledge from information?

2. How might the individuals working on knowledge transfer in your organization better understand the distinctions between explicit, implicit, and tacit knowledge?

3. Who are the deeply smart employees in your organization?

4. How do you know? If asked what makes them so valuable, how would you characterize the cognitive and behavioral processes that constitute their know-how?

5. How could you use the deep smarts indicators to distinguish between experts and competent colleagues?

6. How could you use the indicators to help new hires develop expertise?

7. If you face any unpredictable or unprecedented situations with which your in-house experts have no experience, how can you utilize their critical-thinking processes rather than their pattern recognition?

## Questions for Knowledge Recipients

1. What dimensions of deep smarts are your strongest? Which do you feel need further development?

2. How could you more deliberately accumulate the experiences that will be critical in developing your own deep smarts?

# 3

# Setting Up Knowledge Transfer: The Players Involved

One of us was sitting on the forty-fourth floor of a large steel company headquarters, eating lunch with the top nine officers of the firm. At one point, the CEO leaned over and confided that he was about to fire a small team.

"What would be the best way to do that?" he inquired.

"What do they do?" the visitor asked.

"Um, they are Advanced Sales."

"And what does Advanced Sales do?"

The CEO looked uncomfortable at the question.

"Anwar," he said to the CTO, "please explain what Advanced Sales does."

The CTO squirmed a bit. He glanced around the table for help. Everyone suddenly seemed to find their luncheon plates particularly fascinating.

"Mary," the CTO said, picking on the executive vice president of HR, "why don't you explain what Advanced Sales does."

Mary was just as clueless as the other eight people.

If the top nine people in this multi-billion-dollar company don't know what a group does, that team can't be important, right? The team's *cost* is obvious—right there in the budget. Its value, in this case, was invisible.

A cursory exploration of the team's work turned up an interesting story. Through his extensive contacts, the team member whose geographic region included Washington, D.C., discovered that a piece of legislation slowly but steadily progressing through Congress would require steel with much higher corrosion resistance in residential furnace flues. Seeing the potential to dominate this profitable market, the team member arranged for the company's nuclear division, which already produced such steel, to provide it to the residential division. The moment the bill was signed into law, the company was ready to move on the market—a full two years ahead of its competition. With that one piece of advance sales knowledge, the team member paid for the entire group's salaries for a decade.

As suggested by this story, deep smarts can go totally unnoticed—until they are critically needed, or gone. The following lament posted in response to a *Wall Street Journal* blog is a heartfelt caution to managers:

> *More than one time after leaving a job in the last 25-plus years, I heard through various grapevines that I couldn't be replaced or that no one knew how I did things, or that I had taken with me some magic/secret to getting the day-to-day done. I have no magic or secret. In all of these cases, my co-workers or supervisor did not know what the day-to-day work was, or thought it was boring, or just assumed that I was on top of it. So of course when I left, they were confused. Managers: there is probably someone on your team you depend on to deliver the heavy lifting or the tedious or the complex. You don't give it much thought because you know he/she can handle it, and you don't have to worry about it. You are making yourself and your team vulnerable.*[1]

So who is making *your* team vulnerable? And who (besides you) would care? Regardless of the specific situation requiring knowledge transfer (normal job transitions, retirements, mergers, onboarding), we must coordinate the efforts of four groups of people: stakeholders, knowledge experts, knowledge learners, and facilitators or coaches.

## Who Cares? Stakeholders

The stakeholders include anyone who will need to make knowledge transfer happen, help it happen, or let it happen. They have some vested interest in the outcome of the initiative and probably need to contribute some resources. They can range from the board of directors bringing in a new CEO to the vice president of engineering whose technical ranks are about to be decimated by a wave of retirements. Or maybe the job transition is much less dramatic and the stakeholders are the HR personnel responsible for smooth and effective succession planning at all levels in the organization. The individuals who are feeling (or anticipating) the pain of losing deep smarts may not be the same ones who control the resources needed to carry out a knowledge-transfer program. (See chapter 9 for some suggestions for bringing that latter group along.)

In our survey of CIOs, CTOs, and HR executives, for those organizations with a program to transfer expertise, responsibility for setting it up was spread fairly evenly among different stakeholder departments. Most frequently, HR took the lead role, but in numerous cases, information technology personnel, engineering departments, a special knowledge management department, or a combination of these groups was reported as responsible. Whoever the stakeholders, they will need to understand the costs of losing knowledge and hence the benefits of avoiding them. They will also need to be involved in the "contract," a formal agreement about knowledge transfer between experts and learners, discussed later in this chapter.

# Who Knows? Knowledge Experts

In the previous chapter, we discussed the cognitive, behavioral, and physical components of deep smarts. The goal now is to identify who in the organization has the kinds of deep smarts that are critical to capture, diffuse, or transfer. These individuals are the sources of the knowledge to be transferred. They may be subject-matter experts, such as scientists, engineers, or financial wizards; departing executives; team members (possibly geographically dispersed); and even recent hires or consultants bringing new or emerging knowledge to the organization.

If you know exactly what knowledge to target for transfer or sharing, you can skip to the next section of the book. But wait—are you sure that you have it identified? First you have to be confident that you understand what know-how, skills, and other capabilities underlie your company's success, now and five years from now. Then you have to know how much of that knowledge is in people's heads and hands, rather than captured in standards, processes, and equipment. Next you have to figure out whose heads contain the un-captured know-how. And finally you have to figure out how much of that knowledge is vulnerable to loss during a variety of possible transitions: potential retirements, rapid turnover, mergers, globalization. Or what if someone holding an essential role has no backup and goes bear hunting with a water pistol?

Who knows where the most critical knowledge resides in the organization? The heads of businesses or divisions in a large organization are probably absolutely certain that the individuals in *their* bailiwicks are more valuable than those other people down the hall. And not all managers have the same view as to which skills will be needed in the future. For this reason, organizations need systemic ways of identifying critical knowledge. No single method of identifying the most critical deep smarts can be totally objective, as each relies, to varying degrees, on fallible humans, with their agendas, biases, and quirks. At the same time, each of the following approaches has its strengths: the quantitative analysis of the engineer that creates consensus around numbers; the networker's diagrams that lay out in graphic form for all to see the critical knowledge nodes; the deductive approach of the survey researcher, who starts with a tested theory of what constitutes essential competencies; and the upper managers, who make judgments based on overall strategic objectives.

## By the Numbers: The Engineer's Approach

Engineers love to work with numbers. So one approach that appeals to technical organizations is to present the identification of knowledge at risk of loss as a quantifiable choice. Baker Hughes, a more than $20 billion company that provides drilling, formation evaluation, production, and reservoir consulting services to oil and gas companies, operates in over ninety countries. It therefore has a large contingent of technical experts among their more than sixty thousand employees, as well as people with specialized knowledge about geographic regions. In 2007, Wesley Vestal, currently HR director for Baker Hughes Integrated Operations, worked with then-colleagues Meta Rousseau and Phil Perry at Baker Hughes Drill Bits to set up an internal program called RELAY, whose primary purpose was to rapidly transfer and continue developing mission-critical knowledge and skills.[2] The process was highly structured and started with a *knowledge vulnerability analysis*.

Baker Hughes managers were asked to develop specific, measurable criteria deemed critical to the business. For example, would a vacancy cause the organization to miss revenue or profit projections or customer satisfaction scores? The managers then narrowed the number of critical knowledge roles by evaluating role criticality against the *current* and *immediate* objectives of the business and consequent talent needs. For example, new-customer acquisition might be the most important objective in one business unit, whereas cost reduction might be the focus of another unit.

Next, managers were asked to rate the criticality of that role were it to be lost. For example, Baker Hughes asked managers in various business units to rate "the perceived pain losing the person in this role would cause in being able to perform critical processes [the role] is responsible for" on a scale of 1 to 25. Finally, that person was assigned a number to indicate time vulnerability:

1 = Someone likely to remain in the role for at least two years

3 = Six months to two years remaining until a need for replacement

5 = Potential vacancy in six months or less, or the person could leave at any time

A cumulative score above a specific cutoff alerted the company to the need to capture and transfer the individual's knowledge and led to a concentrated program of knowledge transfer. (A very similar process was followed by GE, as described in chapter 8.)

## *Organizational Network Analysis*

Organizational network analysis (also called social network analysis), as the name implies, makes patterns of informal interactions visible by mapping who collaborates with whom, and to whom colleagues go for help and advice (see the sidebar "Automating Organizational Network Analysis" for an example of a company that is embedding this technique in software). In an R&D division in a large life sciences organization, each of twenty-six hundred employees identified the colleagues they turned to for help for specific critical competencies. The analysis helped the organization determine those technical competencies where hiring efforts should be directed, as well as identifying the current go-to people. But because collaborative skills are not always visible, their value may not be appreciated, with potentially harmful results. One organizational network analysis of a company found that 10 percent of employees in a network

# Automating Organizational Network Analysis

In the future, organizational network analysis for the purpose of enhancing knowledge flows may become quite automated, rather than relying on employee surveys. A startup company, Declara, provides a dramatic example of such automation. The company has created algorithms that attempt to simulate the mind of founder Ramona Pierson. Her highly unusual ability to conceive of cognitive maps was pushed to an extreme when she was blinded and very nearly killed while jogging, by a drunken driver. Her innate abilities became essential to living with new disabilities. She decided to try to embed in software her own extraordinary abilities to navigate within a cognitive map of the world, including social and professional networks. Declara's system links everyone in an organization and learns to identify individuals through their social interactions, the types of questions they are seeking to answer, and who responds best. The software flags people who excel at certain tasks and the go-to individuals whose expertise is most sought by others for particular kinds of information and guidance.[a]

a. Ashlee Vance, "Ramona Pierson Got Run Over, Went into a Coma, Woke Up Blind, and Is Launching One of the Most Original Tech Companies in Years," *Bloomberg Businessweek*, September 30–October 6, 2013, 86–90.

supported 37 percent of collaborations. Yet "more than half of these individuals had not been on senior leaders' and human resource managers' radar screens as employees who played an important role in connecting people across the organization."[3] Such underappreciated people are at increased risk of leaving, taking their collaborative skills and other deep smarts with them.

## The Deep-Smarts Survey Approach

After we wrote the book *Deep Smarts* in 2005, we conducted a study using a survey instrument that was designed to distinguish between people with approximately equal experience, those possessed of deep smarts, and those who might be competent but did not demonstrate an equal amount of expertise. (For details, see the sidebar "Survey of Deep Smarts at a Large Software Company.") It was a useful identification instrument when peers, supervisors, or upper management who knew the work of the individuals targeted for the study were surveyed—but not when individuals rated themselves. As we will see

# Survey of Deep Smarts at a Large Software Company

Several years ago, two of us (Dorothy and Walter) were asked by a large software company ("LSC") to identify people in the organization with deep smarts. Three senior managers examined the dimensions of deep smarts and then nominated pairs of people, matched on age and experience. One member of each pair was to fit closely the deep-smarts profile; the other to serve as a control. We interviewed each of the nominees (we were blind as to which category they were in), as well as each person's direct supervisor and one or two coworkers. All four groups of respondents—senior managers, target subjects, direct supervisors, and peers—completed our forty-item questionnaire measuring the various dimensions of deep smarts, in each case rating the target respondents.

We found that all dimensions correlated significantly with overall deep smarts for all four groups, but three stood out: (1) critical later in this book, self-report measures such as this almost inevitably run afoul of self-presentation biases, and this survey proved to be no exception—pretty much everyone considered himself or herself deeply smart. Surveys that measure expertise are certainly possible, but these instruments are far more useful when completed by others who know the individuals and their work well.

## Upper Management's Approach

Surely, top management is best equipped to direct attention to the deep smarts of the organization, right? If you recall this chapter's

skills and knowledge; (2) systems thinking; and (3) rapid, wise decision making and judgment. There was strong agreement among senior managers, direct supervisors, and peers on which nominees scored high and which scored low on deep smarts.

We also asked our target respondents' senior managers, direct supervisors, and one or two peers to evaluate the target's contribution to LSC. All three groups saw a very strong connection between the nominees' deep smarts and their contributions to the company. The three groups of raters also *strongly agreed with one another* about which people contributed most. We therefore feel reasonably confident that—at least at LSC— we successfully measured deep smarts, and that deeply smart employees are more valuable to the organization than their less expert colleagues. But—and it's a big but—the assessment was *not* valid for the individuals' ratings of themselves! We concluded that if you want to assess someone's deep smarts, don't ask them—ask their coworkers.

opening story about the CEO and his team who had no idea what his advance sales team did, you will be skeptical of that statement. Another interesting finding in the LSC study described in the sidebar was that the upper managers' ratings generally, but not always, agreed with those of the other raters. In fact, in two cases, the ratings were opposite those of the target individuals' direct supervisors and peers, as well as our own impressions after our interviews. All of us thought Mr. X, whom upper management considered deeply smart, was not, and we all agreed that Mr. Y, whom management dismissed, had deep reservoirs of expertise. Cocky Mr. X was more intent on impressing than on delivering considered responses to our questions, and deliberate, soft-spoken Mr. Y was very thorough and thoughtful—hence a bit slower in speaking. Our conclusion at the end of the study, when we discovered the discrepancy between upper management's judgment and that of the rest of us? Mr. X was smart at impressing upward in the organization, and Mr. Y was not—but the latter was the one with more valuable stuff in his head.

There may be no single best method for identifying experience-based, business-critical knowledge. In an ideal world, you would employ different ways and trust that they would yield similar results. In reality, the technique that best fits your organizational culture will probably suffice, but keep in mind the limitations discussed earlier.

## Who Needs to Know? Knowledge Learners

Who wants and needs the knowledge? This could be the incoming executive, other team members, would-be subject-matter experts, potential managerial successors, colleagues—anyone who needs to learn some of the deep smarts in someone else's head. It might seem obvious who these learners are—but make these assumptions at your peril. Just as there are experts who may be flying below the radar, so are there potential successors who could benefit from knowledge transfer but who may not be the first to come to mind.

Matching learners to experts cannot be done casually. The learners must be motivated to work with the expert and, as will be discussed, also need some foundational knowledge to build on.

Moreover, learners often have expertise of their own, in a different knowledge domain. The CEO of the company may be a brilliant strategist who knows the industry very well after twenty years of work. But in transferring some of that knowledge to a potential successor, the CEO discovers that the learner knows a lot more about marketing in Southeast Asia than the CEO does. The successor's questions about current outsourcing policies provoke a lively discussion about their hidden costs. So while we talk about expert and learner, we recognize that at any given moment, the roles may reverse. Moreover, expert and learner are sometimes individuals and sometimes groups. Knowledge can flow from one person to another, from one to several, or from many to many. Regardless of how many people are involved, however, the principles of knowledge-transfer design covered in this book apply across all these permutations.

## *Receptors*

*Mind the gap!* If you've been to London, you'll recognize the warning to be cautious exiting the trains in the Underground because of the gap between train and platform. The warning applies to knowledge sharing as well. Even the best-planned knowledge-transfer process can founder if planners fail to assess the knowledge gap that may exist between an incumbent and the intended successors, between experts and learners. Before you attempt to pour some knowledge into a learner's head, you need to consider what's in there already. Think about your own brain. It's crammed full of memories, mental models, facts, and figures. The information based on your formal education may exist as facts (e.g., the date of the Great Recession), static pictures (e.g., a photo of a neuron), or algorithms (e.g., the equation for calculating net present value). Whatever the form, those memories establish templates or receptors on which you continue to build throughout your life. This tendency to aggregate knowledge into manageable chunks is very useful when you want to retrieve it, add to it, or act on it. But if you lack a receptor to receive incoming information, if there is no "hook" to which you can attach a new admonition, suggestion, fact, or experience—the information can breeze through your mind, leaving no trace behind.

Whether learners have receptors for a particular morsel of knowledge has nothing to do with intelligence and everything to do with experience—what is already in their heads. Even with a lifetime of rich experience, we all lack many receptors. If we ask you what avatar you want in the next MMORPG you enter, would you be able to tell us? You know what an avatar is, and you might know about massively multiplayer online role-playing games—especially if you have teens in your house. But those teens, if they play, will have in their heads a host of experiences that you are unlikely to share. They have visual and spatial memories of the last game played, and they know whether it's better to be an elf or a human in a particular session of *World of Warcraft*. You don't—unless you are a gamer yourself. If a would-be learner, or successor, lacks receptors for the knowledge another intends to impart, the transmission is unlikely to succeed. Every profession has its own jargon, and comprehension of the language is the most basic of receptors. But receptors involve more than terminology.

Experts always find it difficult to explain how they do their magic, because so much of their wisdom is based on tacit knowledge and judgment. When the intended recipient of knowledge has scant receptors, or the gap is large, the task can be extremely frustrating to both expert and novice. An expert chef we know was asked in a desperate phone call from his son to explain how to make the turkey gravy the young man had volunteered to provide for a holiday feast with friends. The chef started to explain but, within a few sentences, realized that his explanation was totally beyond the grasp of the novice at the other end of the phone line. How much flour relative to stock ("Stock! What's that?") or to the drippings in the pan? How long to simmer the mixture? How to keep it from clumping? How to explain about siphoning off grease so you can see how much to retain? The chef gave up in despair: "It's too complicated to explain over the phone." Then a "journeyman" took over the explanation and laid out simple steps, knowing that the resulting gravy would never approximate the texture and taste of the chef's, but that the novice's gravy would be good—and certainly better than what he could create without any guidance. And so it proved; the dinner guests were complimentary. (Not surprisingly, the chef has been teased for years after the event about abandoning his son.)

Everyone—incumbents and possible successors alike—tends to underestimate the extent that judgment and experience-based know-how are involved in a job. New hires can be especially dismissive. Surely, the newly minted MBA reasons, she could be the chief financial officer of the large company in a couple of years. Otherwise, why did she take all those courses in accounting and finance? What she fails to realize is how wide the gap is between the courses and their application in the real world. As recounted to us, a large manufacturing firm discovered the importance of the knowledge gap when managers attempted to link thirty-year veterans directly with apprentices out of the ranks of new graduates. The experiment didn't work, because the knowledge gap was so large. Some experts soldiered on, but they found that they needed to narrow the gap with a lot of remedial education about manufacturing processes, as well as some hands-on experience with the assembly line before they could share their deep smarts.

Sometimes, understanding the *wrong* receptors in people's heads can lead to a more successful transfer of knowledge, as is illustrated in the sidebar "Wrong Receptors: False Knowledge."

## Who Helps? Facilitators and Coaches

Who guides the knowledge-sharing process? Who elicits the knowledge through interviews? Some situations require no third party.

## Wrong Receptors: False Knowledge

Suppose you are managing a team of creatives in an advertising agency and you want the team members to appreciate the importance of *creative abrasion* (the stimulation of creativity through intellectual and cognitive diversity) in arriving at an innovative ad campaign. One of the most common errors made by proponents of brainstorming is the assertion that group members must be uncritical of the ideas generated by one another—that quantity, not quality, of ideas is the most important determinant of creativity, at least in the idea-generation phase of the process. In fact, numerous research studies have demonstrated that groups composed for creative abrasion and who freely critique and debate one another's suggestions arrive at the most creative solutions.[a]

A study of middle-school physics teachers found that the teachers most able to predict the *wrong* answers given by their students (e.g., that it's colder in winter because the earth is further away from the sun) were best able to help the students learn.[b] Similarly, the group leader who understands the value of creative abrasion and knows that most group members probably believe in uncritical brainstorming enjoys an advantage. Such a leader will be more likely to encourage the productive intellectual disagreement that will result in enhanced creativity.

a. Jonah Lehrer, "Groupthink: The Brainstorming Myth," *New Yorker*, January 30, 2012, www.newyorker.com/reporting/2012/01/30/120130fa_fact_lehrer.

b. Peter Reuell, "Understanding Student Weaknesses," *Harvard Gazette*, April 30, 2013, http://news.harvard.edu/gazette/story/2013/04/understanding-student-weaknesses.

However, even when expert and learner are working together in a relationship focused on knowledge transfer (mentoring, apprenticeships, joint projects) some conscious attention to the transfer *process* is needed. This focus can take two very different forms, requiring different skills: facilitation and coaching.

Facilitators guide knowledge elicitation, sometimes with the help of the kinds of question kits described in chapter 4 and sometimes through skilled improvisation, as explained in chapter 5. In either case, facilitators focus on helping the knowledge flow from experts to learners and on structuring the discussion so that the output can be captured.

Coaches also need to keep the knowledge flowing, but they focus more on removing any organizational or interpersonal barriers that might impede that flow. The role varies somewhat among organizations. Knowledge-sharing coaches are senior people with credibility in the organization. Their main job is to maintain the momentum of knowledge transfer by monitoring progress and intervening if necessary to identify resources. What all knowledge-sharing coaches have in common is their understanding of how their own organization works and their responsibility for helping the transfer occur.

Both the facilitator and the coach roles can be assumed by internal or external consultants, but the coach role is much more effective if undertaken by an internal player. We will discuss the tools and techniques in detail later, but for now, note that some players must specifically devote energy to knowledge transfer. In many, if not most, cases, knowledge does not automatically flow without some kind of facilitation or coaching. At Bank of America, which uses both coaches and facilitators, the coach is a peer mentor (see the sidebar "Bank of America's Onboarding Program for New Executives").

## "Are We All Agreed Here?" The Contract

In the early 2000s, a team of internal and external consultants at Pfizer developed a process for retaining critical knowledge in its

# Bank of America's Onboarding Program for New Executives

Bank of America has recognized the need to ensure that leaders get off to a fast start as well as the need to reduce the high rate of failure among newly hired or internally transitioning executives. To address these needs, the bank has created an onboarding program for executives one to two levels below the C-suite. The program aims to ensure that the new executives understand role expectations, quickly develop a network among key stakeholders, build relationships with their team, and learn from other leaders what it takes to succeed, especially in their particular role. To achieve these objectives, the program must transfer not only explicit knowledge, but also implicit cultural knowledge and unwritten norms. Three elements of the program are briefly described here: an onboarding plan or navigational guide, the appointment and training of a peer coach, and a dialogue between the new executives and their direct reports, managed by a trained facilitator.

The onboarding plan identifies both formal and informal stakeholders (ten to fifteen managers, peers, business partners, and direct reports) who can provide critical knowledge about the organization, including cultural norms, and who can subsequently review and assess the performance of the new executive over the first two years of employment. The objectives of the plan are to clearly lay out the roles of the peer coach and stakeholders and steps the new executive can take to manage the transition, including building necessary relationships and adapting to the culture. The plan also identifies archival materials that would be useful for the incoming executive.

A successful colleague employed at the bank for at least two years is appointed as a peer coach; he or she will have an extensive professional network and significant experience in the area of the business the new executive is entering. The coach is responsible for meeting regularly with the newcomer, explaining expectations, serving as a sounding board for any issues that may arise, providing feedback and guidance, and offering candid information about the organization, including unwritten rules and possible challenges to expect in the new role. For example, one unwritten norm critical for a successful entry into the organization is the need to build strong lateral relationships that cross several boundaries, such as geography, functions, and line of businesses. For their part, the new leaders are expected to actively query their peer coaches about lessons learned, factors that have led to success, and what the coaches wish they had known when they started working at Bank of America.

A third element of onboarding is a facilitated integration session held within the first thirty to sixty days of entry. The facilitator is a leadership development executive who has a deep understanding of the leader's business issues and is familiar with the specific leadership team's interpersonal dynamics. The facilitator first meets separately with the team to gather data on such issues as what the new leader needs to know about the inherited leadership team and the challenges that the new leader will face. Team members may also raise questions that they would like to have addressed by the new leader, such as management style and aspects of the new leader's experience or background that have not been already described to them. The facilitator then shuttles this information back to the new leader, to prepare him or her for

the discussion with the team. The discussion ends with agreement on action items, issues to be addressed in the future, and
sometimes a team-building exercise.[a]

a. Joe Bonito, senior vice president, leadership development, Bank of America,
interview with the authors (DL, WS), August 5, 2013.

R&D division, which was concerned about a rising tide of retirements and other transitions. Each transition begins with a contract
that identifies the key stakeholders who will take ownership of the
process, and specifies key objectives. The process has been used successfully in scores of situations since, including internal promotions
and departures of key experts. The only failures have occurred
when neither the stakeholder nor the learner (successor) engages
with the process.[4]

Without some prior agreement about objectives, resources, and responsibilities, knowledge transfer can resemble a relay race with runners attempting to pass the baton across different lanes, even toward
different finish lines. Some of the most common issues to be resolved
ahead of time involve resource allocation, including time. For example:

- The expert and learner are excited about working together—
  until the learner's boss stipulates they can do so only on their
  own time. (Do you prefer Sundays? Friday evenings after nine?)
  And how about resources such as travel funds? Dream on.

- The learner, an incoming executive, discovers that the incumbent, who is going to work for a competitor, is leaving
  two weeks before the replacement's arrival date. No overlap
  between the two of them has been allotted. None.

- A community of practice was set up to develop and share
  knowledge among geographically dispersed experts.

However, the sponsor has left, the community of practice has few resources, and people have drifted away to focus on the jobs they're being paid for. The community has been deemed a failure by management; meanwhile, the company struggles to deal with problems that afflict its far-flung enterprises.

Setting up a written, if not formal, agreement about knowledge sharing may strike you as a bureaucratic impulse best ignored—wait awhile until the urge passes. But doesn't it make sense to agree on a destination before you start on a journey? And well intentioned as the participants may be, it's not enough for an expert to agree in principle to share knowledge and for a successor (or successors) to desire to learn. A signed (yes, actually signed) agreement that acknowledges the desired end goal spells out, at least at a high level, the methods by which the knowledge is to be shared and the time it is likely to take above and beyond normal work hours is enormously useful. The bosses of both experts and learners have to be signatories to the agreement, thus acknowledging that the knowledge transfer is worth an investment and agreeing to provide the necessary time and resources. When viewed as an add-on to an already impossibly crowded work schedule, any knowledge-sharing initiative is a nonstarter. The agreement doesn't have to be called a contract, of course. That term conjures up mental pictures of legal forms to be signed in quadruplicate. The important point is that those who control the time and other resources necessary for a successful knowledge-sharing program need to officially buy into the plan. For an example of an actual contract, see the GE Global Research Centers story in chapter 8.

The initial contract need not involve a huge initiative. Change can start small and focus initially on areas where there is great need—pain points—and a good likelihood of a quick, affirming success. And there are some relatively easy and inexpensive ways of harvesting the know-how within reach. We will show you some in the next chapter.

## Questions for Managers

1. What methods of identifying deeply smart experts would best suit your organizational culture?

2. If there are such experts relatively low in the organizational hierarchy whose knowledge is important to operations but who go unheralded, how could these individuals best be identified?

3. What methods are being used in your organization to identify likely successors for important roles? How could you help such individuals develop the necessary receptors and learn more actively from experts?

4. Who could facilitate knowledge transfer between experts and learners?

5. Who has the budget and interest to sign off on knowledge-transfer efforts? How could you use the costs of knowledge loss identified in chapter 1 to bring these people along as stakeholders?

6. Which other stakeholders in your organization might see the value in knowledge transfer?

## Questions for Knowledge Recipients

1. Who are the deeply smart people in your organization? How could you capture knowledge from these experts?

2. How do you know if you have adequate receptors to effectively capture the experts' deep smarts? How might you acquire the necessary foundational knowledge to build those receptors?

# PART TWO

# Tools and Techniques

THE REST OF the book provides an overview of many knowledge-transfer processes, derived from our own experience and that of others who are intimately and daily involved in knowledge sharing. We start with the simplest and least time- and training-intensive and work our way to the most challenging—but most rewarding—tools and techniques. In this part of the book, we also suggest ways to track and monitor the transfer process—the closing of the initial knowledge gap between experts and learners. We take you into the heart of a transfer program conducted at GE's Global Research Centers. And finally, we focus on what you will need to do to clear the way in your organization for whatever knowledge-transfer action you decide to initiate.

# 4

# Smart Questioning

The dean of Arts and Sciences at a large university has just left to become provost elsewhere. "Pierre" has been promoted to take his place. Pierre has had several administrative positions, including department chair, so he feels well qualified for the position. However, as he sits in the (much more comfortable) chair at his new desk, he sees a number of mystifying notations placed on his calendar by his administrative assistant.

"Er, Helen, what is this meeting every Tuesday with the ITRC?"

"I think that stands for Information Technology Resource Committee."

"Who is on that?"

"Sorry, I don't know. I think it's in one of those files Daniel left you."

"Do you know what the committee does?"

"Um, no, but you are the chair."

"Oh. Of course. How about the appointment tomorrow with this fellow, Georg von Seldon?"

"He's from Switzerland. He wants to follow up on planning for a faculty exchange program that's been in the works for a while."

This kind of dialogue goes on for a half hour. Pierre realizes he is going to have to telephone his predecessor. The job description he was given during orientation sure didn't cover all he's going to need to know.

Pierre knows from *whom* he needs to learn—and a fair amount about *what knowledge* he needs. But how does someone in this predicament proceed? And can he set up a process that will aid his own eventual successor?

## Learn to Fish, or Hire a Fisherman

There are two basic strategies organizations take to address loss of knowledge and productivity during transitions. First, you can "learn to fish," by trial and error and learning as you go. Second, you can "hire a fisherman"—a knowledge-transfer consultant. Expert "fishermen" can either do the work of knowledge transfer for you, with little or no transfer of their own deep smarts, or train you to do what they do, integrating their deep smarts about knowledge transfer into your organization. (You'll see a detailed description of that process in chapter 8.) This book is intended to help you with either of these strategies. If you select the first—to go fishing yourself, you will want some guidance steering you toward some promising fishing holes. And if you hire a fisherman, we aim to give you a head start thinking about what—and how—you would want to learn. With either strategy, you will need to consider specific techniques for eliciting and transferring the deep smarts you have targeted to preserve.

## Matching Your Situation to Transfer Techniques

There are two primary considerations in selecting knowledge-transfer techniques: how urgent the situation is (i.e., the amount of time you have to complete the transfer), and how much of the knowledge to be transferred is implicit or tacit, versus already explicit. Let's explore these two considerations.

## Urgency: How Much Time Do You Have?

An organization is fortunate when there is enough time for an incumbent to work with a successor, but the sudden departure of a critical employee is common. People's lives take unexpected turns, and they leave the organization with little advance notice. Or there is a reorganization and a sudden shift in roles. When there is sufficient bench depth, these departures present no problem. But when time is of the essence, you can use the smart questioning (knowledge-elicitation) techniques suggested in this and the following chapter to conduct exit interviews that dive much deeper into the knowledge than is typical of most such efforts. The more time available, the wider the range of techniques covered in this book that you can apply.

## Type of Knowledge: How Much Is Implicit or Tacit?

A second determinant of knowledge-sharing techniques is the extent to which the deep smarts you want to retain or rebuild are still in the head of the departing expert—not documented and possibly even unconscious. As we discussed earlier, there may be filing cabinets—physical or digital—filled with explicit knowledge: job descriptions, reports, presentations, articles, process documentation. And these can be very valuable. But technical experts, whether in finance, marketing, or software design, have process notes in their heads. And even the affectionately known gearheads from technical strongholds such as Caltech or the Indian Institutes of Technology often have so-called soft skills: project leadership or other management tasks that rely on cognitive or sensory dimensions of deep smarts. Those, of course, are *never* written down.

Taken together, these two considerations (urgency and type of knowledge) determine what techniques of knowledge capture and

FIGURE 4-1

## Two primary determinants of knowledge-sharing initiatives

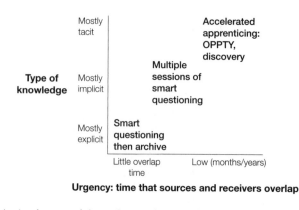

Urgency: time that sources and receivers overlap

OPPTY: a structured process of observation, practice, partnering and joint problem solving, and taking responsibility.

transfer are most effective (figure 4-1). In the next three chapters, we discuss various ways of eliciting and capturing knowledge, making sense of it, and then massaging it into a form that can be transferred. In this chapter, we start with the bottom-left part of figure 4-1, covering urgent situations, when the time available for knowledge transfer is relatively short. In such time-constrained situations, the goal is to transfer primarily explicit but also some implicit knowledge. In chapter 5, we assume that more time is available and that the focus can shift to transferring more of the implicit and perhaps making explicit some tacit dimensions of the experts' deep smarts. And in chapter 6, we concentrate more on tacit knowledge, which can be re-created through accelerated experience and discovery exercises.

# Eliciting Explicit and Implicit Knowledge

Knowledge elicitation is a bit like eating an artichoke. You start with the explicit, move on to the implicit, and probably uncover some tacit knowledge in the process. You also start with the broader, more comprehensive categories of knowledge and then look deeply within each category—moving ever closer to the heart of deep smarts.

Many of the examples of smart questioning in this chapter involve one-to-one transfers (expert to learner; incumbent to successor) or one-to-many (an expert or experienced executive transferring knowledge to more than one successor), but smart questioning also facilitates many-to-many exchanges, as when members of teams or communities of practice share among themselves. Whether the objective is to *capture* and archive expertise for the benefit of future (possibly unknown) users or to *transfer* as much know-how as possible to identified successors, eliciting knowledge through smart questioning is a powerful technique for both purposes, In fact, it is also useful in the accelerated apprenticeships we will describe in chapter 6. The common steps in peeling the knowledge artichoke for all these purposes are enumerated in figure 4-2 and guide the discussion in this chapter.

FIGURE 4-2

## Steps in knowledge elicitation

**Describing the role of the expert**
Identify primary tasks, roles,
responsibilities

↓

**Targeting deep smarts**
Identify/confirm knowledge domains to be
targeted

↓

**Identifying areas of implicit and tacit knowledge within targets**
Judgment; uncertainty; risk; unique skills

↓

**Smart questioning**
Use templates or structured
narratives

↓

**Reporting or archiving**
Check on accuracy and completeness; customize presentation to use

## *Role of the Expert*

So what does the expert do all day, week, year? A formal job description usually captures only part of a person's responsibilities; many of those responsibilities and tasks associated with the role are implicit, having never been written down or perhaps even discussed. There are numerous ways of capturing the details of an individual's work life, but one is to create a very detailed and complete job description in a visual map.

The company Transition-Path creates such maps, which they call BroadScopes. Working remotely, an analyst asks an executive or a subject-matter expert sitting in front of his or her own office computer screen a series of ever more detailed questions. The responses are captured in a map that evolves in real time before the respondent's eyes, laying out what he or she does, starting with the most prominent uses of the respondent's time. These "buckets" are usually four to seven major categories of activities (see figure 4-3 for an example).

Next the analyst asks the respondent to focus on each of these major categories in turn to explore them at some depth, to make connections where activities are interdependent and to flag those that are particularly important. For example, what tasks could fall through the cracks if he or she departed, or which functions carry a

**FIGURE 4-3**

**Visual map of one expert's BroadScope of his major activities**

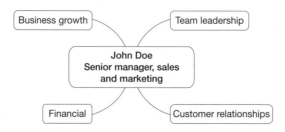

*Note*: The process of creating a BroadScope was developed by the firm Transition-Path to lay out, in ever-increasing detail, an expert's capabilities.

**FIGURE 4-4**

## Detail: John Doe's business growth activities

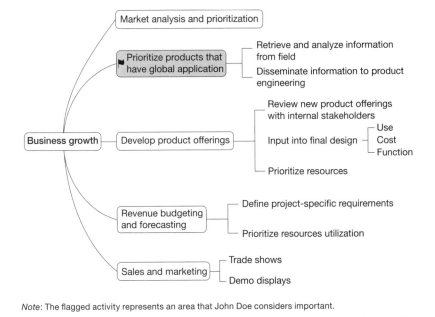

*Note*: The flagged activity represents an area that John Doe considers important.

special risk to the organization if not done well? See figure 4-4 for an example of how just one of the main categories has been expanded. (This example is simplified so it can be read on a book page.)

Transition-Path CEO Brian Monette reports that a common reaction when all the tasks, responsibilities, and roles are laid out for a busy executive or subject-matter expert is "Wow! I didn't realize all I was doing." The full maps often have to be printed out on large sheets, because the respondents provide so much detail that the map can become unreadable. The flag in figure 4-4 indicates an area where John Doe must exercise judgment; it represents what he considers especially important and potentially at risk if not done well. The flag also suggests an area to be probed for deep smarts. (We will describe later how we do this for the activity flagged as mission-critical in the figure: "Prioritize products that have global application.")

In addition to being very satisfying to the respondent's ego, the resultant map is useful for a number of purposes, especially for a potential successor. Because, as noted earlier, a job tends to grow with the person (competent people attract ever wider responsibilities), the work displayed on a map may be split into separate jobs and for more than one successor. But however the work will be divided after the executive or technical wizard leaves, the map provides an easily accessed visual document of where expertise may lie.

## Targeting Deep Smarts

Once we know all the tasks, activities, and responsibilities an individual undertakes, we can decide which of those roles and tasks can be probed to provide a better understanding of the know-how at work. That is, we can assess just which skills, capabilities, and behaviors make the executives or wizards so valuable to the organization. We move from *what* the individual does to *how* he or she does it—where the deep smarts lie. Not everything in the head of an experienced subject-matter expert or executive need be transferred. Anyone with that much experience has numerous possible knowledge domains, some of which might be essential to the business, but other skills or responsibilities might be deemed routine, outdated, or otherwise considered poor candidates for transfer. So which aspect of that person's experience-based knowledge is critical to the organization? This question embodies our shorthand definition of deep smarts. The first task is to identify those critical functions or, if they are already known, to confirm them. So, for example, a departing general manager might have responsibility both for sales and for leading company growth. However, if there is a very strong sales manager to step up as a successor, the company might decide to focus on how the general manager has set growth strategy and balanced safety issues with cost-cutting initiatives.

## *Identifying and Confirming Areas of Implicit and Tacit Knowledge within the Deep Smarts*

Experienced executives will sometimes protest that as they are not subject-matter experts, they have little knowledge to pass along. They do not recognize that they are valued not so much for *what* they know, such as details about current products or services, as for *how* they make decisions, diagnose tricky situations, manage teams, or represent the organization in public forums—their cognitive and behavioral deep smarts. Some of their know-how may be explicit—already captured in reports, training manuals, or other documents. But there are always areas of implicit and tacit know-how that are unlikely to have been documented. They are often characterized as gray areas, requiring the most judgment and experience; as high-risk areas; or as areas about which the expert possesses unusual or even unique knowledge. Thus, implicit and tacit know-how are identified for further exploration. Here's a sample question designed to begin delving into the individual's deep smarts: Which of the domains, tasks, situations, or processes that are components of your job fit the following descriptions?

- They require extensive, personal experience.

- They require the most judgment, or represent gray areas in decision making.

- They entail the most risk for the organization, were they to be done inadequately.

So, for example, in the case of John Doe, whose BroadScope of his business-growth-related activities we saw in figure 4-4, we might focus on the flagged section "Prioritize products that have global application." John has marked this activity as particularly important, and it clearly involves judgment. We would want to investigate just how John goes about selecting and rating such products.

This seems like a possible gray area. What are his criteria? How are they weighted? Does he do any market testing, and if so, how? Does he seek advice from any particular individuals within or outside the firm? The products and customers of the future may be very different, but the development of good criteria for global marketing, including research and testing, is likely to apply well into the future. That's what we are after—the deep smarts that have value across time and situations.

## Questioning: Who Asks, and What to Ask

As any reporter, counselor, lawyer, or police investigator could tell us, questioning is an art, sharpened through experience. But we don't always have experienced questioners available—and in some situations, they wouldn't be needed, because the nature of the problem or situation to be addressed dictates the form of the question. Table 4-1 describes knowledge-elicitation techniques associated with various situations, starting with those in which a specific problem requires a quick response, and therefore accuracy is more important than subtlety or craft in formulating the inquiry.

TABLE 4-1

**Knowledge-elicitation techniques requiring relatively little training**

| Knowledge-elicitation technique | Suggested application situation: what is the need? | Potential output |
| --- | --- | --- |
| **Just-in-time sharing** | Urgent need to solve specific problem; access to some form of community of practice | Solution to question; based on peer experience |
| **Exit interview** | Capture some (limited) guidelines for a successor | Rules of thumb; identification of priorities/problems |
| **Questions using templates or question kits** | Capture of implicit knowledge by successors or lightly trained questioners | Archives; personal extendable data bases; examples, cautionary tales |

## Just-in-Time Sharing: Throwing a Bottle into the Pond—or Ocean

Say you have a problem you can't figure out, and there's a fellow down the hall who knows a whole lot more than you do about this area. So you pop in, pose the question, and spend some time picking his brain. You emerge with some possible solutions in hand. Such informal, just-in-time knowledge sharing goes on all the time, but some organizational cultures are much more accommodating than others. At Agilent Technologies, for example, the culture allows for a variety of such informal knowledge-elicitation opportunities. Some experts have set up office hours, just like instructors in a university, when any knowledge seeker may bring in a question or problem. Others with a similar reputation for wisdom have an open door—no specified hours, but an invitation to ask for a consultation anytime. Still others have deliberately set up a kind of coffee break where people with questions can accidentally-on-purpose bump into experts for a conversation. Very little (besides an encouraging boss and willing experts) is required to set up such models. Even less, other than time, is required of the knowledge seeker to pose the question or the expert to address it.

Now let's raise the level of complexity a bit. Organizations or individuals who need knowledge *right now* are usually seeking an answer to a pressing question. But instead of having an expert down the hall, they don't know who will have the best answer, although the population who might have it may be limited to a set of peers or more experienced colleagues. So it's a pond, not the ocean, into which the bottled question is thrown. Of course, the question has to be well framed, but this kind of knowledge elicitation—like informal chats—requires little training, just access to the network of folks who are thought to have the required knowledge. In some models, the knowledge is typically shared in face-to-face meetings; in other models, remote sharing is more usual. Furthermore, the sharing can occur in real time or be archived and accessed as needed.

Communities of practice have evolved in part to respond to just-in-time knowledge inquiries. Their networks, often connecting people across the globe, require some form of electronic system to support the knowledge sharing. Setting up the knowledge network and the user interface may be extremely complex, requiring great skill to make the interface user friendly and the reach comprehensive enough, but once the network and supporting infrastructure

## Just-in-Time Knowledge Sharing in the US Military

The advantages of just-in-time knowledge sharing gained prominence during the Iraq War, when midlevel field officers were faced with unprecedented challenges, such as avoiding injuries and deaths from improvised explosive devices (IEDs)—simply constructed, lethal weapons placed along roadsides, in animal carcasses, or behind road signs and posters. By the time the normal channels of disseminating knowledge were pursued—identifying the need, sending it up the chain of command, and, sometime later, receiving a response—conditions on the ground would have evolved and the advice would have been useless. The real experts were the men and women who were encountering the IEDs in the field, either directly and, tragically, through near misses, or from stories and intelligence. But how could such knowledge be passed along to where—and when—it was most needed?

It all started when two majors, Nate Allen and Tony Burgess, who had been friends at West Point, found themselves next-door neighbors in Hawaii. They spent many hours on Allen's front porch sharing their experiences and problem-solving techniques, which they then used to deal with issues in their own battalions. They posted their observations in an online book, which attracted exist, little skill is required of the questioner to elicit the desired knowledge. As we will see in chapter 7, many of the communities of practice have proven the value of the capital expenses required to connect knowledge seekers with experts.

The US military has its own form of such a community, and the payback is not just in cost savings, but also in lives saved (see the sidebar "Just-in-Time Knowledge Sharing in the US Military").

the attention of a captain at West Point who, journalist Dan Baum explains, "was familiar with a website called [AllOutdoor.com]. On this site, sportsmen post questions and solicit advice about everything from how to skin a squirrel by yanking on its tail to how to call a turkey."[a] What appealed to Allen and Burgess was the real-time, unfiltered exchange of information and advice from users of the site. Using AllOutdoor.com as a model, they subsequently created two websites to enable real-time exchanges of information and advice among officers: Companycommand.com, for use by captains, and Platoonleader.org, designed for lieutenants.

West Point subsequently put both Companycommand.com and Platoonleader.org on its server. A third site, Cav.net, was developed soon after. It was intended to assist patrols in the field when they were facing immediate threats within the next patrol six to nine hours out—such as grenades wired behind posters, which would detonate when soldiers ripped the posters down. This kind of just-in-time information saved lives. Lieutenant Keith Wilson warned his men after seeing a "be on the lookout" posting—and a soldier sent to take down a poster cautiously looked behind it first. "Sure enough, a grenade was waiting."

a. Dan Baum, "Battle Lessons: What the Generals Don't Know," *New Yorker*, January 17, 2005, 42–48.

But deep smarts also exist across the globe in pockets not tied into a particular organization or community of practice. There are increasingly few barriers to accessing them through just-in-time questioning. One of the great advantages of the World Wide Web is the opportunity to seek, identify, and utilize expertise outside our own organizations. The *Idea Connection Innovation Newsletter* is one of well over a dozen such free online publications that allow contributors to post requests for innovative solutions and to publicize new ideas. The publications perform a service similar to the problem-solving outreach employed by communities of practice and other in-house requests for expertise.[1]

Whether the knowledge lies within or outside the organizational boundaries, the process we are talking about still largely applies. People still have to go through the basic steps of figuring out the valuable parts of the knowledge and deciding how to transfer it.

### Generic Questioning: The (In)famous Exit Interview

The term *exit interview* evokes images of someone pursuing a departing expert out the door, waving a sheet of questions. Many exit interviews are taken seriously, recorded and archived for future reference, and actually used. But many more are perfunctory or ignored. Possibly the greatest virtue of a traditional exit interview is that little questioning training is required if there is a standard set of questions in place. We might suggest that there is commensurately less lasting value to the knowledge uncovered, however. Few organizations that we know of have the kind of built-in aids to those conducting exit interviews—aids that well-designed communities of practice have for members seeking answers to problems. Exit interviews are therefore highly variable in quality. The better ones reflect the skill of the individual doing the questioning as well as the thoroughness of the questions.

Baker Hughes has used three types of exit interviews, depending on the time constraints and criticality of the role: If time was limited, the role was very critical, and a lot of people needed to tap into the knowledge, a panel-led interview would be conducted. The panel would include experts, potential successors, and managers as recommended by the retiring expert. If more time was available and the role was less critical, either an individual technical exit interview or a "traditional" exit interview would be conducted. The first two types were more like knowledge-elicitation sessions, but there were some topics that were asked of everyone, such as: "What are the ten hardest problems you face on a regular basis? If you had one day to brief your replacement, what would you discuss?"[2]

Sometimes, a superior exit interview can be based on a few thoughtful questions, with responses about selected activities carefully probed to elicit the most useful knowledge. In a large international study of knowledge management, Holly Baxter, chief scientist at Strategic Knowledge Solutions, identified many best practices, including the three questions asked of departing personnel in one organization:

1. What are three things you have learned that you wish you had known when you started your job?

2. What is the biggest challenge your replacement will face? What advice would you give them?

3. What are the two initiatives/knowledge products you are most proud of? What made/makes them effective?[3]

Responses to questions like these are obviously highly situation-specific and require follow-up probes to be really useful. Imagine receiving this parting (rather cryptic) instruction from a highly experienced kiln operator in a lime production facility, in response to a query about advice to a successor: "Watch out for when she [the kiln] starts making high kind of squeaking noises; you probably need to take her off-line for a few minutes." If the successor is not present to find out what a high squeak sounds like and how long "she" should rest, it could be tough to use that information!

A risk assessment manager we know in a global operation was a bit more helpful. In his exit interview, he suggested that his successor make time to visit every foreign operation at least once a year and ask what the local manager is doing to monitor expense accounts: "Some cultures assume that expenses we consider as personal are legitimate business costs, but we really can't allow them." Better yet, the questioner asked for examples of nonpermissible expenses to include in the archived interview. One was charging travel and entertainment expenses without any evident business purpose. The successor is now alert for such behaviors that could lead to charges of fraud.

### Knowledge Elicitation Using Question Kits or Templates

Research on, and the practice of, knowledge transfer has progressed to the point that we now recognize the major topics of importance to the potential successors of experts. Templates or question kits that reflect these topics can be useful shorthand guides to eliciting knowledge. The templates can vary somewhat, depending, for example, on whether the expert is a scientist, an engineer, or a high-level manager, but in general, the categories are widely applicable.

The Leonard-Barton Group, with K.L. Hagen and Associates, has created a set of standard question kits for learners to use during and after the knowledge-transfer workshops that consultants lead. These kits address issues within predetermined categories. Table 4-2 provides a sampling of categories with a few illustrative questions for subject-matter experts and follow-up probes. You could use these or similar categories and develop your own questions—which would differ for managerial roles.

Question kits are most valuable when the individuals involved are motivated to learn from the experts, but need a starting point and some structure to follow. With a little bit of training, a motivated questioner can successfully elicit a fair amount of knowledge in a very short time. This is not to say that *no* training is necessary.

TABLE 4-2

## Sample question kit for knowledge elicitation

| Subject of question kit | Sample questions | Probes or requests for examples |
|---|---|---|
| Foundational knowledge | What reference materials do you use?<br><br>How do you track technical trends? | Should a knowledge recipient own any of these reference materials? What are the best websites? Are there particular journals that you find useful? What about associations? |
| Professional network | Whom do you contact for information about government regulations?<br><br>Whom do you ask about technology trends and innovation? | What is this go-to person's complete contact information?<br><br>What medium does he or she prefer (email versus telephone)?<br><br>What is his or her background?<br><br>How do you know this person? |
| Technical/ scientific | What kinds of problems do people come to you to solve?<br><br>What are the biggest risks in the project, process, or system you manage? | Can you describe a problem brought to you recently? What technical mistakes is a novice likely to make in that project or process? |
| Organizational | Who are the major stakeholders in the project, process, or system you manage?<br><br>What are the biggest mistakes newcomers make in trying to get projects going here? | What are the positions of the major stakeholders? Where are there competing priorities?<br><br>Can you give me an example of a newcomer mistake and suggest how to avoid such mistakes? |
| Customer | What value do we add to our biggest customer's business?<br><br>What problems have we run into in serving them? | What is the best way of presenting that value? Can you give an example?<br><br>Tell me the history of those problems, how they were solved, and by whom. |
| Interpersonal | Regarding team leadership, what criteria do you use to select team members?<br><br>How do you ensure the team is connected to the overall business strategy?<br><br>On a general level, how do you motivate people who report to you? | Why do you use these particular criteria?<br><br>Have you ever chosen unwisely?<br><br>What communication strategies are most effective?<br><br>Can you give an example of what has really helped? |

The more that the questioners know about the nature of implicit knowledge, the more alert they are to important nuances and to interesting responses that might not fit into an obvious category. And questioners usually do need to learn to ask probing follow-up questions. Unless asked, interviewees tend to give vague explanations or make comments that beg for a follow-up probe. "You have to know how the system works," an interviewee might say. Or "we never did that again." The most powerful follow-up questions to such general comments are: "Why?" and "Please give me an example." The kits have been successfully used either as onetime knowledge-capture mechanisms or as structured ways to help learners gather knowledge over time from experts.

The answers to the questions in such kits are only as insightful as the questioner and the people responding. Here's an example of a good exchange. A learner asked an expert in a technical organization, "What problems have we run into when dealing with customer X?" The expert replied with a story about a serious problem once encountered in the field with a particular product and how it was resolved over a holiday weekend with heroic actions by the account manager, working with the firm's top engineers. The manager went to the home of the chief operations officer in the customer company to show what was being done to resolve the issue—a gesture very much appreciated by the customer. The expert summed up: "Always be completely honest about failures, but always go to the customer with a solution." Sound advice. (Notice that the example ended with a rule of thumb, which makes the story more generally applicable.)

There are at least two advantages to using templates. The first is scope—which translates into speed. K.L. Hagen and Associates was once asked to help a large pharmaceutical company figure out which projects and personnel from a newly purchased competitor should be retained. With the deadline for completion of the merger just six months away, a great deal of knowledge identification and transfer was required in short order. Who better to do that than the five hundred scientists and researchers who would be responsible after the merger for the compounds the acquired company had been working on? Mobilizing these individuals solved the problem of covering so much ground so quickly, and they were certainly technically qualified. But however brilliant these individuals were, they lacked experience in eliciting knowledge. They needed help to do so efficiently. And this illustrates the second advantage to using templates. The consultants created standardized sets of questions and templates, somewhat customized for different groups, to reflect where the product, program, or process was in the development cycle, from invention to implementation.

## Customizing Question Templates

Experienced facilitators often adapt their question templates to processes already familiar to the experts and learners, so that the elicitation seems less foreign. In the previous example of the pharmaceutical company, the templates were based on a product review process familiar to both companies and adapted to production processes and development. A set of questions often adapted to other uses is the well-known US Army's After Action Review (AAR), which was originally created to identify lessons learned and ways to improve performance. Knowledge-transfer consultant Kent Greenes has adapted an AAR-type exercise to knowledge transfer, as when he was asked by British Petroleum to help a refinery crew. There was a major crew change under way (60 percent of employees were going to leave within the next two years), and knowledge was not getting transferred at the crew level. The younger workers thought they knew enough from their training courses, the veterans didn't feel comfortable sharing their experience without being asked, and there was little time to spare for anything but work. Greenes opted to have the crews conduct AARs as a natural part of the job.

At a natural break in the work, or immediately after the end of a shift, Greenes would ask the workers to pause to answer some questions about some issue, for example:

- What was supposed to happen? *The convection section in a hydrogen furnace was to be removed.*

- What actually happened? *The convection section was unable to be removed because of structural problems. We lost six hours of work.*

- Why were there differences? *When the support members were cut, the walls collapsed and bricks fell down into the piping. Had to shore up and cut ten feet off north and south ends to reduce weight.*

- What can we do for the next task or job that will make an improvement? *Anticipate that steel members are fatigued and not as strong in older equipment. Add more support and use more trolleys. Support side walls with turnbuckles to prevent brickwork from falling.*

When these AARs were conducted, knowledge was transferred, without any perceived preaching. The two groups learned together. Though much of the knowledge was coming from the more experienced crew members, the process was accepted as a fast way for everyone to learn what was relevant, a routine through which knowledge was generated and transferred in context.

The three elicitation techniques in table 4-1 (just-in-time sharing, exit interviews, and questions in templates) that we have just illustrated are not only easier to administer than other techniques, but also somewhat easier to analyze and make sense of, because the form of the question basically dictates analysis. That is, the responses to the questions are slotted into existing categories. New categories can be derived from responses to question templates, but the templates offer a built-in organizing system.

Just-in-time shared knowledge often goes into an existing data repository. Exit interviews are usually the responsibility of HR departments, which archive them in idiosyncratic ways, including video libraries. The output from question kits and templates is reported or archived in various ways as well. Sometimes, individual learners are responsible for their own compilations. However, in other cases, as when findings from a number of questioners are being synthesized, a summary report goes to the primary stakeholders. In all these cases, the archived repositories are potentially available to knowledge seekers, including (in the case of exit interviews) future successors.

There is no one best way to archive knowledge, and of course, much depends on capture methods and resources available. But many huge archives have gone virtually unused because more attention was paid to knowledge capture or its comprehensiveness than to subsequent ease of access by the intended or actual end user.

In some just-in-time sharing systems, the responses to questions undergo an extensive checking and classification process. For example, at ConocoPhillips, its "Ask and Discuss" sessions on a particular topic are closed after sixty days. The closed discussion item (CDI) goes through a review by knowledge leadership before being archived for subsequent use. Identified knowledge leaders are responsible for flagging highly relevant CDIs for "PDF-ing": creating PDF files with attachments that provide a snapshot of the valuable CDI for later reference. If the intellectual capital is highly pertinent, a wiki article is written and placed on the internal wiki network. The entire process promotes very fluid knowledge sharing that can be continually referenced and added to.[4]

So now you have peeled back one layer of leaves of the artichoke. But if you want to get closer to the heart, to capture some of that marvelous experience-based know-how that makes an expert so valuable, you will want to use different—or additional—techniques. And unless you have some experience yourself in finding and extracting the critical threads out of a mass of tangled narrative, you may want some guidance. The following chapters provide some of that guidance.

## Questions for Managers

1. Where is there urgent need for knowledge capture in your organization? Just how urgent is it? That is, how much time do you have?

2. How could you document all the tasks, responsibilities, and activities undertaken by a person in a given role so that you can decide which of those a successor (or successors) might need or wish to take over? How will you determine if there could be more than one learner matched to a particular expert?

3. How do you figure out within those tasks, responsibilities, and activities exactly which aspects of the incumbent's deep smarts could and should be targeted for transfer? That is, which are most critical to the organization? Who is making that decision?

4. How much of that knowledge is explicit, implicit, or tacit? Which of the knowledge-elicitation approaches described in this chapter would be most applicable?

5. Who could do the questioning? Could some individuals be provided with templates to assist smart questioning?

6. How can experts in your organization be made available for just-in-time knowledge sharing through electronic or in-person communication?

7. How seriously does your organization take the exit interview when seasoned managers or technical staff members leave? How could you make the exit process more strategic and detailed, and could the results of the process be made more accessible to successors?

8. In your organization, is there a small group of highly valued experts who have a particular role and whose collective wisdom could be captured in best practices and diffused to less experienced colleagues?

## Questions for Knowledge Recipients

1. How could you include some form of active knowledge elicitation in your own development plan?

2. How well does your job description cover all that you actually do? What activities and responsibilities would you like to take on, either to do your job better or to expand your role?

3. If your organization conducts exit interviews of departing experts, can you access those that have been archived? Could you sit in on some?

5

# Capturing Deep
# Smarts—with Help

One of us (Dorothy), with many years of interviewing experience, was working with a colleague less experienced in the art. She conducted some interviews together, and then he did several on his own. The results were a bit frustrating—not as useful for the intended purpose of capturing deep smarts. "I think I'm asking the same questions you are," he said. "How come I don't get the same kind of responses?" There were probably two reasons: first, he was more of an expert than she was in that particular knowledge domain. This should make it easier, right? No. He knew so much about the topic that he made automatic connections of his own, assumptions about what the interviewee meant. And second, he knew the individual being interviewed personally. It seemed rude to ask a probing follow-up question, as if he somehow didn't believe the first response he got. Both of these reasons conspired to make the interviews somewhat superficial, touching only the surface of the topic. The interviewer was not unintelligent—far from it. But he didn't have the distance or the discipline to dig deeply.

For all the reasons we have explained, the most valuable know-how does not lie at the surface. When deeply smart people are interviewed, they tend to make sweeping generalizations, to fall back on jargon to explain, and to get impatient with questions that appear to ask about the obvious. So it is often easier for a facilitator from outside the immediate work group to ask the "dumb" questions that reveal the reasoning, to insist on examples to illustrate what the interviewee means, to probe for more details.

The categories in table 5-1, stories or histories, peer sharing, and deep-smarts interviews, all generally require more skilled facilitation than the three elicitation techniques we discussed in chapter 4. Although we are still talking about smart questioning, the interviewers in these situations require more experience. Lacking a template or an obvious set of questions, the interviewer must frequently improvise, organizing and structuring the inquiry on the fly, taking note of the responses that require follow-up probes without interrupting the respondent to the degree that he or she loses the train of thought. All this while simultaneously capturing the interview output in some form. In the case of an expert sharing a narrative with a group, facilitation is even more challenging, as the facilitator

TABLE 5-1

## Knowledge-elicitation techniques requiring training and experience

| Knowledge-elicitation technique | Suggested application situation: what is the need? | Potential output |
|---|---|---|
| Structured narratives: critical incidents; histories | Capture critical thinking of experts; capture practices in process or system | Cognitive maps; process/systems maps |
| Facilitated peer sharing: peer assists; knowledge jams | Diffuse known solutions; combine disparate perspectives | Action plans; creation or transfer of solutions |
| Deep-smarts interviews, validated by peer interviews | Capture best practices, including critical thinking, of technical experts and experienced executives | Expert's skills enumerated and described, in text and/or cognitive maps |

has to keep the group on track while structuring the ongoing flow of the knowledge sharing. And in some of the following suggested techniques, the facilitator also serves as scribe for the whole group, structuring the notes publicly in front of everyone, so that the group members can see where they have been and what areas of discussion remain to be explored.

Again, we structure the chapter from relatively easily facilitated inquiry to more difficult. Let's begin with eliciting stories from deeply smart people.

## Structured Stories for Knowledge Elicitation

Stories are memorable. Humans have been telling them since we lived in caves, and stories have always helped us teach, learn, and remember. Therefore, narratives are very useful vehicles for transferring knowledge.[1] Part of the reason harks back to the nature of knowledge. Stories create pictures in our minds, give rich context and detail, build receptors, and provide vicarious experience. Of course, the most valuable ones for knowledge transfer are those deliberately chosen for relevance (e.g., stories likely to reveal the expert's judgment and critical decision making) and structured for efficient, effective analysis.

Facilitators often find that the most effective way to gather data from stories that can be analyzed for implicit and tacit dimensions of knowledge and passed along to learners is to elicit details in a relatively free-form way, with few preconceptions about what patterns will emerge. The complex narratives of successes and failures that executives and subject-matter experts have experienced over many years, or particular incidents that illustrate the expert in action, are rich veins for revealing critical thinking and for eliciting the best practices in a particular process or situation. Moreover, when used with groups, knowledge elicitation through stories enables participants not only to participate in the questioning but also to take away whatever parts of the vicarious experience are most relevant for them personally. And best of all, group members enjoy such sessions. As he was leaving a critical-incident review session, a very senior executive commented: "This is the best training process I have seen; I learn best from stories." We think most people would agree.

## Critical Incidents

Look at the *Wall Street Journal* almost any day, and you will see a story about an incident—good or bad—to which corporations had to respond. The stock market Flash Crash of May 6, 2010, a product recall by GM or Toyota, the commercialization of 3-D printing in a particular industry—in organizations literally around the world, such an event triggers internal actions and often requires the judgment and response of organizational experts. Systematically walking through the history with experts who were on the ground floor coping with the crisis reveals much implicit knowledge—what resources they called on, where they sought the best information, what were the criteria for selecting particular responses, what alternatives the experts considered, and with whom they communicated and why. This kind of walk-through is a rich vicarious experience for whoever is hearing the story and learning from it. Not being the expert decision makers themselves, the audience will have had a more limited viewpoint, without understanding all the complexities of the context. Moreover, if the audience goes through several such incidents with the same expert or set of experts, patterns of thinking and acting that were repeatedly applied begin to surface. Such patterns provide a model for others to consider in future situations.

### Selecting Incidents: Recent, Relevant, Revealing

The incidents selected for a walk-through should be recent enough that the expert can remember relevant details; important enough that serious choices had to be made; and complex enough that those decisions revealed judgment and the application of deep smarts. For example, one retiring executive whose deep smarts were to be transferred had wide responsibilities, broad experience, and a very extensive network of information sources inside and outside the firm. The stakeholders therefore decided to start with a variety of situations: (1) an important crisis to which the incumbent skillfully responded; (2) an example of his creativity in initiating a program that greatly benefited the firm; and (3) his handling of a recurring, serious client problem. Giving the expert some advance warning about the incidents to be covered allowed him time to review pertinent documents and refresh events in his mind.

Who should be responsible for selecting the critical incidents that will be explored with the expert? The experts themselves are

## Illustrative Questions to Be Asked in Selecting Critical Incidents

To the expert or executive:

- What are some critical events from which you have learned much?

- Which of these events illustrated situations and decision-making requirements that you believe anyone in your position should be able to handle?

- Which would be most helpful to potential successors?

- Are these recent enough in your memory that you could provide details about how you made your decisions, whom you involved, and what alternatives were considered and rejected?

To upper management:

- In what critical events, situations, or organizational processes has this expert played a major role?

- Where have you seen his or her judgment and capabilities best illustrated?

- Which critical events would illustrate the skills or deep smarts you want the organization to preserve?

To potential successors (if known):

- In what critical events, situations, or organizational processes have you seen the expert demonstrate superior judgment or decision making?

- Which of these events or processes have left you wondering about the expert's underlying reasoning or the resources he or she used (including contacts), and about which you would like to ask questions?

not always the best, or at least the only, stakeholders who should be involved. Upper management often has particular skills in mind that it would like surfaced through the narratives. Successors have their own priorities and will recall incidents they have observed deftly handled by the expert, wishing they understood the underlying logic and decision-making criteria. The sidebar "Illustrative Questions to Be Asked in Selecting Critical Incidents" suggests some questions from the perspective of experts, upper management, and learners that may be used to decide which critical incidents will make useful stories for eliciting knowledge. You will undoubtedly think of others.

## Facilitation Techniques: Literally Writing on the Wall

Once the critical incident has been identified, it is helpful for the facilitator to have some guiding questions in mind. The questions are deliberately open-ended and generic, but provide some structure to what otherwise can devolve into a rambling narrative. Filling out a timeline and probing for the reasons behind each decision builds the anatomy. Such sessions are best conducted in a room with lots of writing space, so that a full timeline can be drawn for all to see. Writing space is also needed for the responses to questions such as those suggested by the following critical-event protocol or those from the assembled group members. If the facilitator is technically agile, the timeline can be captured electronically, but the capability to go back and fill in additional details as they emerge in discussion is vital. Moreover, having the whole timeline visible allows the group to note interactions and interdependencies. For that reason, the best technologies for capture are old-fashioned whiteboards— or even a wall covered with paper. Of all the facilitated knowledge-elicitation approaches, this technique is the most accessible and easily implemented. A skilled facilitator—even one without specific training in knowledge transfer—can be highly effective. But we do suggest that a template helps. The template presented in the sidebar "Critical-Event Protocol," used by the Leonard-Barton Group as a guide in examining critical incidents, is a good place to start.

Let us look at an example, necessarily extremely truncated because of space considerations, but nonetheless briefly noting the major elements of the outlined protocol. If we were looking at this incident in real time, we would cover a four-by-ten-foot whiteboard with writing—and if we reproduced that here, you would require a microscope (not just a magnifying glass) to read it. So we have chosen just a few important decisions. Moreover, if we looked at this event from the federal government's point of view, rather than from the New York Transit Authority's, we would have many dozens more decisions to highlight—and literally hundreds of actors.

# Critical-Event Protocol

1. Start with the event:

    a. What happened?

    b. Who was initially involved? What was your role as an expert?

    c. What were the immediate consequences of the event?

2. Create a timeline with key decision points or actions noted—before and after the main event. At each decision point, ask the following questions, as applicable:

    a. Who was involved?

    b. What was the decision?

    c. What action resulted? (Sometimes, the decision and the action are indistinguishable.)

    d. Were alternative actions or decisions considered? If so, why were they rejected?

    e. Provide context: What events, situations, or environmental issues outside the actors' control had an influence? (Often includes competitors' actions.)

    f. For some decisions: What assumptions or expectations existed at that point?

        i. Who made these assumptions or had these expectations?

        ii. Were they tested?

        iii. Were the assumptions or expectations wrong or right?

    g. For some decisions: What cues or signals were important to note?

## Critical-Event Example: New York City and Hurricane Sandy

In October 2012, Hurricane Sandy devastated the Eastern Seaboard of the United States. New York City was particularly hard hit.[2] During the time leading up to the storm's arrival, a number of people made some very wise decisions. On October 19, when Sandy was still a tropical depression, CEO of New York Transit, Thomas Prendergast, had cots, bedding, food, and water moved to temporary shelters where he knew track workers, train crews, carpenters, and bus drivers might have to stay, unable to return home, if the hurricane hit the city. Governor Cuomo decided to close down the whole New York subway system when Sandy was reported to be moving up the coast, and the governor announced it was time to take action. A relatively minor player in the drama made what turned out to be a literally life- and property-saving decision. Engineer Frank Jezycki was responsible for a dam being constructed at the 148th Street Station in East Harlem to hold back the Harlem River. When he inspected it, he ordered that the dam be raised and strengthened. This decision proved to be critical, because the Harlem River runs toward Lower Manhattan and could have flooded the parts of the subway system that were used by more than 1.8 million people every day. When the river rose during the storm, it came within three inches of topping the dam.

The various heads of the Metropolitan Transportation Authority (MTA) sections began meeting hourly. It fell to them to decide what to do when Con Edison was forced to shut down a plant, leaving half of the city without power. The fact that the outage affected only half of the city was actually more problematic than when the whole city was blacked out (in a prior incident), because half the subway train terminals were not functional. The trains coming in from the Bronx, Queens, and Upper Manhattan had nowhere to turn around. Commuters needed to get to work—into and back out of the city. The problem was solved by setting up temporary terminals where no trains had ever been turned around before. Implementing this decision drew on the collective knowledge of everyone who knew the electrical power

FIGURE 5-1

Highlights from the New York Metropolitan Transportation Authority (MTA) response to Hurricane Sandy

| OCT. 2012 | 22 | 28 | 29 | 30 | | | Nov. 1 |
|---|---|---|---|---|---|---|---|
| Context | Tropical depression | Moving up coast | Sandy hits | Con Ed shuts 14th St. Station | Half-city outage | Regular terminals no power | No way to get Midtown |
| | 660 miles of track | | Harlem River huge threat | | | Power problems unprecedented | |
| Who | CEO Prendergast | Gov. Cuomo | Frank Jezycki | Heads of MTA transit sections | | | Police |
| Decision | "Can't wait" | Close MTA | Dam 148th inadequate | Meet hourly | | Create "bus bridge" | Create bus zone |
| Action | Materials for dam sent | Worker camp set up | Height increased to 8.5 ft. | Adapted fast-track methods | | 1,100 buses on routes 1,000 bus staff working | |
| Result | | Workers live 24/7 | Dam holds | Swift recovery | | Commuters able to get to work and back | |

systems. The group in the control center also set up a "bus bridge" to ferry commuters to those parts of the subway that could be used.

Of interest to us is the demonstration of judgment, swift decision making, and very deep smarts about the system under threat. Dozens of decisions besides those just named were made by experienced maintenance and operations employees. The response of the MTA to the crisis was remarkable; other cities have learned a great deal about preparing for and dealing with natural disasters from being walked through this incident. Figure 5-1 shows, in highly abbreviated form, parts of this critical event and how it was handled.

## Project Histories and Reviews

Stories used for knowledge elicitation need not be about disasters or other adverse events to be extremely useful. Project histories can be very effective vehicles for transferring knowledge from experts to learners or among members of a team who may not have identical background experience. Again, the main purposes are not just to list decision points, but also to understand the reasoning underlying each decision. In the case of product or service histories, why were they designed as they were? Did competitor actions, technological advances, or events in the marketplace at the time influence decisions? Responses to such questions help the designers of current products or services in numerous ways. By learning which designs were considered and encouraged or rejected in the past, current designers avoid thinking that some design solutions were simply overlooked, rather than deliberately rejected for good reason.

Similarly, research project reviews can provide a context for colleagues not involved in the original research or can demonstrate to less experienced researchers how their more expert colleagues diagnose and solve problems. For example, a multinational medical device company that had developed a number of miniaturized life-saving implantable devices was faced with an increasingly common problem: so many of the scientists who had developed the technologies had retired that key knowledge was held by only a few people. New hires, while very talented, lacked the personal experience and organizational memory of their predecessors. As a result, there was redundant work and repetition of past mistakes. Although some explicit knowledge was being captured, the deep smarts of the retiring experts were not being transferred. K.L. Hagen and Associates were brought in to help identify, organize, and transfer the critical, specialized knowledge held by one retiring expert, who was continually called upon by corporate scientific teams for his knowledge of past work. Through interviews with him, the consultants identified the critical events and breakthrough moments, rationale for decisions, ideas that worked and were used and those discarded, what he said the scientists wished they had done differently, and how they might apply their insights to current projects. See the sidebar "Sample Questions to Ask in Projects as Stories" for examples of the kinds of questions that can be used to elicit the knowledge of a departing expert.

## Sample Questions to Ask in Projects as Stories

1. How did this project get started, and when? Who have been the major players?

2. What were the major objectives or purposes of the project?

3. What have been the major milestones and events?

4. What alternative solutions or directions were considered and rejected? Why were they not used?

5. What obstacles did you encounter, and how did you move through them?

6. Going forward, what are the greatest risks this project faces? What would a risk-mitigation plan involve?

Besides addressing the original goals to ensure that the expert's departure did not affect development quality and speed, the exercise had several unanticipated benefits. During the presentation of the history to a group of interested employees, a developer who was initially skeptical of the activity identified ideas that could be applied to a current innovation. Additionally, a marketing person discovered that what he had regarded as a threat from a competitor's superior technology actually embodied an approach considered and rejected by his company because of its risky nature.

Making sense of critical incidents, project histories, and other narratives is an inductive process, akin to working from lab reports to diagnose a possible disease or creating a performance review from multiple observations and comments of coworkers. The capture, analysis, and presentation of results are intertwined, because the situations requiring knowledge transfer and the nature of the knowledge itself vary so much. While the experienced facilitator may see some familiar patterns emerging from the observations, this kind of analysis is very open-ended. For this reason, we suggest that both the elicitation process and the analysis of the results require training.

## Sharing Knowledge among Peers

We have focused mostly on a vertical flow of knowledge, from experts to less experienced people. But the flow can also be horizontal— from peer to peer or among colleagues. Such sharing usually involves groups of people and, as with the selection of critical incidents, requires a lot of planning. When peers share knowledge in meetings called for that purpose, skilled facilitators are needed to keep the discussion on track.

### *Onboarding*

As part of its service, executive search firm Caldwell Partners offers a free one-day session of onboarding assistance. An experienced facilitator such as managing partner Jim Bethmann convenes an all-morning inquiry session with the incoming executive's direct reports, scouting out possible pitfalls and issues the new executive should know about. The reports field questions such as "What should Fred know about this company and the product line? What are some major issues he needs to address in sales, operations, and finance? What needs to change? What are the biggest hurdles he will face?" After consolidating responses, Bethmann then brings the new hire in, presents the findings from the morning, and facilitates an open discussion where the direct reports can ask questions of the new hire and vice versa. The session can be tough, as the direct reports may raise questions such as "Why did you take this job? What do you want to do within the first hundred days? Are our jobs safe?" But this process brings issues to the forefront. By the end of the day, Bethmann says, "the doors are open, the veils are gone; there is immediate direct communications." Many potential common problems are ameliorated.

Now here's what those of us who deal with knowledge transfer find discouraging: fewer than 50 percent of Bethmann's C-suite clients take advantage of this facilitated knowledge-sharing service.[3]

## Peer Assists

*Peer assists* are facilitated problem-solving sessions, usually occurring in real time and face-to-face among groups that are confronting similar problems. The objective is to transfer a proven solution from one site to another, although often the different context requires adaptation, as you will see in the following example.

A health-care provider in Alaska was developing a capital business plan that required approval and funding from outside sources. The company's aim was to renew or develop facilities for the aged and grow its capability for long-term health care. Decision makers rejected the preliminary proposal, asking the company to develop a less costly plan. The team had already exhausted knowledge from local resources. Consultant Kent Greenes was brought in to plan and facilitate a peer assist. The peers he contacted were eight health-provider operatives in Washington and Oregon. They met with the Alaska team in Anchorage. By early afternoon of the first day, it was clear that the peers' advice was going to be to reduce costs by remodeling and repairing existing facilities. The recommendation met with resistance from the Alaska team members, who insisted that environmental and customer needs were different from those in their Northwest sister states and that a facelift would not attract, serve, and retain Alaskans needing long-term care.

Part of the planned program was for the peers to visit several long-term care facilities in Anchorage. This was an eye-opening experience—the visitors came to understand the Alaskan context, including climate extremes and patient populations, and changed their advice. The group then spent the second day developing new options and approaches for a new capital plan proposal. One recommendation was to conduct a survey of the target population. A peer from Oregon had recently conducted such a survey and offered a set of questions geared to providing design input for the proposed facilities. On the spot, the peers modified the survey to address the Alaskan context—for example, sensitivity to native Alaskan culture. The peer assist led to a breakthrough; the new proposal was approved and funded. The visiting team benefited as well, and some continue to communicate and collaborate on a routine basis.[4]

## Knowledge Jams

Another type of group exercise focused on knowledge elicitation is what Katrina Pugh calls a *knowledge jam* to emphasize the collaborative nature of the process. The objective is to uncover and capture knowledge to improve some specific process, product, or organizational development project. Group members consist of both knowledge *originators* (executives or subject-matter experts) and *brokers*, whose role is to help pose questions, to learn, and then to implement whatever actions are suggested by the conversations. One of Pugh's clients was the Institute for Healthcare Improvement in Massachusetts, a not-for-profit organization promoting improved health-care delivery throughout the world. The consultants planned a knowledge jam focused on "How do diverse hospital quality team members 'gel' into a team that is a force for change within their organizations?" The knowledge jam originators were nurses, doctors, and quality program managers representing hospital teams varying in how long they took to become productive. Brokers were institute faculty who wished to diffuse the best practices. During the jam, the major insight from the effective teams was "that it is critical to 'gel' intentionally (using process, people, and quality methods), but that informal interactions such as storytelling help them stick together." As a result, the Institute of Healthcare Improvement added "gelling" components to the intervention methodology used across all its health-care delivery organizations.[5]

As noted previously, facilitating such group discussions requires an ability to multitask and to capture the shared knowledge in some written form while simultaneously formulating the questions that move the group forward. Facilitators must be prepared to pull the discussion back into focus, to alert participants to inconsistencies, to dig deeper when possibly essential decisions are glossed over, and to call on individuals whose attempts to contribute are not being heard.

## Deep-Smarts Interviews

The final technique noted in table 5-1 is the creation of an expert or executive portrait that goes far beyond a description of what he or she does to how the individual conducts daily tasks, carries out responsibilities, and has earned the respect of colleagues for extensive know-how. In chapter 4, we wrote about identifying the deep smarts involved in some particular task, responsibility, or activity—deciding which of those would be the most fruitful target for further inquiry. And we suggested a few questions to help you do that. Now we are prepared to uncover not only the implicit knowledge, but also some of the tacit knowledge involved in carrying out the identified task or activity expertly. As discussed earlier, deeply smart people generally have unusual cognitive skills, including technical or managerial know-how. They understand technical or organizational systems, or both, and thus can predict interactions among component parts; are aware of context, which allows them to make fine distinctions; and can diagnose situations and problems better than their peers. Most of these deeply smart people also have some valuable behavioral characteristics: they network extensively with other smart experts; they actively seek cues that will help them identify and test patterns; and they often have both superior interpersonal and communication skills. Some also have special sensory intelligence—tactile (think delicate surgery), visual (think expert interior design), gustatory (think wine expert). Many of these skills can be applied to situations in the future, even if those situations differ from the present—and therefore their transfer has lasting value.

## Interview the Expert

In conducting deep-smarts interviews, successful analysts don't ask about these characteristics directly, however. Rather, they interview with open-ended questions, beginning with a starter kit such as the one shown in the sidebar "Sample Questions for Deep-Smarts Interviews" and following with probes to wherever the expert takes them. Stories and examples continue to be a very important source of information during these interviews. But it is also possible to combine techniques, for example, deep-smarts interviews, followed by separate storytelling sessions focused on critical incidents or product histories and with the active participation of potential successors. The deep-smarts interviews serve to inform the selection of incidents or situations to focus on and provide a broader perspective on the individual experts than the critical incident stories alone.

We tend to make sense of the responses to such questions by clustering the evidence into the deep-smarts categories (table 2-1), at least initially. Of course, not all deeply smart individuals exhibit all of the characteristics. Moreover, some unexpected or even unique themes might become apparent. We realize that like everyone else, we are subject to the "law of dumb expectations," a.k.a. confirmation bias (seeing what you expect—and want—to see). So why use the deep-smarts characteristics as a tentative way of categorizing statements, examples, and stories? Because research and experience

# Sample Questions for Deep-Smarts Interviews

1. What problems do people ask you to solve? Can you provide recent, detailed examples?

2. If people were sent in your place to deal with this task, situation, process, or problem, what would you tell them to look for? What questions should they ask?

3. How do you know if the task, situation, process, or problem is being handled well?

4. What mistakes does a novice make when addressing this task, situation, process, or problem? Can you give examples?

5. Can you tell me a story of when you handled this task, situation, process, or problem very well? Walk me through what happened.

6. Can you give me an example of when this task, situation, process, or problem did *not* go well?

(ours and those of others) suggest that at least some of those characteristics will be present, and noting them will help us make sense of otherwise undifferentiated input. The deep smarts of subject-matter experts and executives tend to cluster in different ways, as you would expect. (For example, executives tend to demonstrate strong leadership and other behavioral smarts more often than do subject-matter experts, whose deep smarts may be more technical.) But we always think of the categories as hypotheses so that we don't force some idiosyncratic capability under an inappropriate heading. And fitting the observations to the deep-smarts categories when they do obviously apply aids in communicating what we observe.

To see how using the categories works, let's look at two examples of deep-smarts interviews, again greatly abbreviated. In the first, the objective was to capture some of the deep smarts of a fire behavior specialist who had been working on planned wild-land fires for the US Forest Service for decades and was nearing retirement age. James Steele's experience-based knowledge complemented the analytical, computer-based models used to predict wild-land fire behavior. The second example looks at "José's" expertise in sales and marketing in a beverage company.

One example of Steele's ability to anticipate events not covered by the usual models was his predicting the sudden reignition of a fire that had been supposedly contained. How had he done that? Recalling a specific incident, he explained that there were numerous *heat sinks*, namely, areas where live or dead vegetation or rocks absorbed and preserved heat. Although heat sinks were addressed by models of fire *ignition*, the models ignored the potential for flare-ups in areas already burned over. Such heat sinks were fueled not only by retained heat in rocks but also by certain kinds of shrubs that hold water and didn't catch fire the first time the fire went through but could harbor enough heat to cause hot spots and reignite the fire.

"Species does matter," Steele explained. "I mean, alder can produce a fairly tall shrub in the northern Rockies—six, eight, ten feet tall. That matters inasmuch as it has a very broad leaf, and it's a really dark green. And so it does absorb a lot of heat . . . But it's not as reactive a heat-sinking fuel as things like snowberry, manzanita, ocean spray, nine bark . . . Snowberry [has] very small elliptical leaves that are a light green. But because even the stem material is so small, it heats up quickly . . . [In this specific situation], those things heated up all night long. And so, you know, it didn't take but a little bit of sunshine or a little bit of heat and wind, and the fire moved there really quick."[6]

Steele's experience-based knowledge not only was absent from the computer models, but also included many visual mental images. He found that newer hires, lacking his experience and his knowledge about vegetation, were unable to visualize how a fire would behave in the center of the burning area, not visible from the periphery. Thus they were unable to anticipate when and how a fire supposedly under control could suddenly pose a renewed threat. However, aspects of this implicit knowledge could be passed along, once made explicit.

What did we learn from this and other examples? There are some discrete lessons, to be sure. One might be this: *be aware of the capacity of heat sinks to reignite fires*. But combining this example with others, we find a larger point in light of the deep-smarts framework, a point that could have broader implications for the education of new Forest Service fire behavior analysts. In Steele's stories and explanations, he demonstrated two aspects of deep smarts that we saw frequently among the specialists we interviewed. First was the ability to analyze a fire as a *system*, taking into account interactions among such factors as weather, humidity, terrain, and human interventions in determining fire behavior. Second, he showed how *context* matters—what kinds of flora are present and their characteristics. He and other fire behaviorists argued that the only way to develop these kinds of so-called instincts is to walk around enough to know the territory and to be constantly thinking about what is going on around the part of the fire being focused on. For the Forest Service, one implication is that newbies need to be helped to think about fire behavior as a *system* and to build a repertoire of *contexts* that they can visualize. While we don't want to lose the discrete lessons, we can also help the service make sense of a plethora of examples by synthesizing some of the observations into the categories provided by the deep-smarts framework.

The deep-smarts interviewing approach to knowledge elicitation is useful any time such as this, when a particularly expert individual is leaving the organization or is intending to split his or her duties with others. Another application is when an expert (or several experts) embodies best practices that, once captured and understood, could be diffused throughout the organization. The following is an example of this situation.

We were once asked to conduct deep-smarts interviews to figure out how a particular vice president of sales and marketing in a beverage company was so skillful at his job. "We'd like to clone José," we were told. When we asked José questions such as those in the sidebar "Sample Questions for Deep-Smarts Interviews," he identified a number of technical skills, such as swift analysis of data. He was asked to consult internally whenever there were problems in the interactions among brewers, distributors, and sales outlets. He believed he was good at diagnosing problems with distribution and gave us examples of times when he had seen problems that prior vice presidents of sales had not noticed. These *cognitive* skills are familiar indicators of deep smarts.

He also had considerable *behavioral* and even *sensory* know-how that set him apart from colleagues in sales. For example, while he was insistent on collecting and analyzing data, he also checked possible conclusions with observations from the field. He routinely visited distributors and outlet stores, looking for cues that would inform his decisions and reinforce or disconfirm the data. "I love data, but I also mix the data with retail. I have a very strong belief that you have to be able to touch, see, and feel in order to put a full picture together of what the issues and opportunities actually are." We asked him what he would tell people to do if they were charged (in his absence) with determining how good or bad a distributor was, as that was a typical judgment he was called on to make. He responded with a list of indicators he looked for in sales outlets that would suggest patterns of helpful or bad activities. (This ability belongs in the deep-smarts dimension we've called *diagnostics and cue seeking*.) For example, he looked at whether and how his company's product promotions were displayed. If they were hand-drawn signs

# The Limitations of Self-Report: "If I Work Here, I Must Be Deeply Smart!"

In a study we did with a large software company, we asked two groups of people—those whose senior managers considered them deeply smart, and a matched group of employees judged to be merely competent—to complete a questionnaire designed to assess their levels of deep smarts. Direct supervisors and peers had no trouble accurately differentiating between the two groups. Perhaps not surprisingly, however, *every individual nominee considered himself or herself equally deeply smart!* There is an extensive literature on the *self-serving bias*, in which people are naturally inclined to present themselves in a positive light, particularly when others might be evaluating them. So, while questionnaires might prove useful as personal, confidential guides to strengths and weaknesses, if you want to get a more accurate assessment of someone's deep smarts, ask someone else who knows the person well.

or poorly placed displays, he knew from experience that he would likely find other patterns indicative of an indifferent distributor.

All of these characteristics were gleaned both from responses to our questions and from numerous examples José gave of how he solved problems, how he worked with distributors, and what he did with his direct reports. All the data he provided was self-reported, however, and we know how fallible such reflections can be (see the sidebar "The Limitations of Self-Report: 'If I Work Here, I Must Be Deeply Smart!'"). So the next step was to talk with some of his direct reports, to validate our conclusions from his responses to our inquiries.

# Sample Questions to Ask Peers about the Expert

1. What makes your colleague particularly skilled at this domain, task, or responsibility? Can you give a specific example of a time when your colleague demonstrated that skill?

2. What does your colleague do differently from others in a similar role or when addressing the same domain, task, or responsibility? Can you give an example?

3. Could a new hire address this domain, task, or responsibility as well as your colleague does? Why, or why not?

4. If you could choose one skill or capability related to this domain, task, or responsibility that you think would be useful for someone to learn from your colleague, what would it be?

5. What know-how would be lost to the organization if your colleague left?

## Validate with a Colleague

We all know that a 360-degree review of performance is likely to reveal some information that the subjects of the review don't know about themselves. That's what makes such reviews so tough—and so useful. As reported in the sidebar "The Limitations of Self-Report," peers and immediate supervisors of the participants in the study at the large software company were better able to sort out who had true deep smarts than were the participants themselves. After all, none of us are immune to certain self-serving convictions about our abilities, such as the statistically impossible but oft-reported belief that we are *all* better-than-average drivers. What we get from the interviews with the experts themselves is not *whether* they are deeply smart (that has already been determined by the organization), but rather an understanding of the experts' own perceptions of the experiences that underlie that expertise. Interviews with peers about a given individual's deep smarts are useful not only for validating what the individual says about himself or herself, but also for expanding on self-observations (see the sidebar "Sample Questions to Ask Peers about the Expert"). The very nature of tacit knowledge is that much of it is not apparent to its possessor, but may be to a careful observer. We have encountered many deeply smart individuals who thought anybody could do what they do—but their colleagues knew better.

In the case of José in the beverage company, his direct reports not only confirmed what we had identified as his deep smarts, but added some. When we asked these peers what he did differently from others in a similar role, their responses were consistent. "He takes unclear or complex situations, and he translates them into actionable next steps." He "gets very tactical, but with an overarching theme." And similarly: "He can think at thirty-five thousand feet one moment and then at a highly detailed level the next."

Some of what we learned about José fit neatly into our deep-smarts framework—for example, his diagnostic skills. But the one skill just mentioned—his ability to shift between the strategic and the tactical—was specific enough to José that it needed to be treated separately in our deep-smarts report. This particular cognitive skill is not found across the board in all deeply smart people. Its identification illustrates why it is important to keep an open mind to deep-smarts characteristics that don't fit readily into our general template but that are important in a particular setting or individual.

Now you have gathered a great deal of information through knowledge-elicitation techniques of one kind or another. The next step is to aggregate all your notes and make sense of them.

## Reporting or Archiving the Results

Communicating the results from knowledge elicitation depends not only on the questioning mode but also on the intended use of the output. Knowledge-elicitation results can be presented either in text, as cognitive maps, or a best-practice process map. Let's look at an example dealing with risk analysis in a financial services company. In highly regulated industries, risk analysis is not only a critical function, but also an area that calls for a lot of expertise and good judgment.

In this firm, a very experienced employee was retiring, and his colleagues needed to understand how he investigated a possible violation of a federal regulation. What emerged from the interviews (conducted with the colleagues in the room so that they could ask questions) was a behavioral process that looked a lot like a detective procedural or legal thriller—no killers lurking in the bushes, but a lot of evidence gathering and interviewing. The investigator first had to compare the actions of the accused violator with the applicable rule. He had to interview the accused to determine what that individual thought (or claimed) he or she was doing, and why. The employee also consulted with colleagues, seeking their opinions about whether this was a clear violation. He sought data about the violation and the violator: when it happened, whether there were mitigating or aggravating circumstances, and—interestingly, just as in the justice system—whether there was a history of prior similar violations.

His real expertise, however, came in his dogged pursuit of the details that confirmed or confuted the original assumption, made by both him and his colleagues, that a violation had actually taken place. He iterated the cycle of gathering data and collecting testimony until

FIGURE 5-2

## Deep-smarts schematic of an investigative process

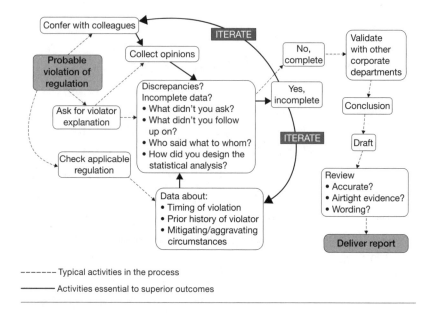

------- Typical activities in the process
——————— Activities essential to superior outcomes

he was certain that he had not neglected to follow up on inconsistencies (figure 5-2). His peers were less tenacious in challenging themselves and others in similar situations. As a consequence, more superficial investigations had sometimes exposed the firm to risk.

The process mapped in figure 5-2 was also presented in text form to the learners. Some individuals tend to prefer text, while others find a visual presentation easier to follow. Not only is this particular schematic more parsimonious than a text description, but it also illustrates the iterative nature of the expert investigator's process better than an admonition to "repeat steps 4 through 8" might. It was also accompanied by specific examples of what he meant by discrepancies, incomplete data, and criteria for satisfactory design of statistical analysis.

So far in our examples, we've been talking mostly about implicit knowledge—that which has not been previously documented or maybe even ever articulated, but which we can mine through smart questioning. We have suggested that you can tap deeper into some tacit knowledge by pulling out stories that provide insights into decision making and critical thinking that the expert may never have consciously examined. By bringing these subterranean mental processes to the surface, you can convert some tacit knowledge to explicit knowledge that can be used by successors. Moreover, involving successors and learners in the process allows for more than capturing deep smarts—some of them are also transferred. In our work both with the financial services company and with José in the beverage company, we used these tools and techniques because we were in a hurry, with only days to capture and transfer knowledge. Yet the very best way for anyone to gain deep smarts is through experience—vicariously, if necessary, but personal experience guided by an expert if at all possible. And the more you exercise your brain muscles in pursuit of knowledge, the smarter you become. In the next chapter, we turn to the techniques for which we personally feel the most enthusiasm. These are the gold standards for the transfer of know-how, because they expand the learner's experience base.

## Questions for Managers

1. What critical events, situations, or projects in the history of your organization have experts handled adroitly? Who would be the best judge of what incidents should be explored? Who was really involved? What did he or she actually do? How were key decisions made, and why? What effect has that history had on today's operations?

2. If there are such critical incidents, who should be involved in documenting them? Do you know all the players whose expert judgment affected the outcome?

3. Which individual experts in your organization possess so much critical knowledge that a deep dive into their expertise is warranted? Are there individuals in the organization who are adequately trained to elicit the knowledge? If not, how could your organization train such individuals?

4. How could you arrange for possible successors to such an expert to participate in knowledge-elicitation sessions, including giving them the opportunity to ask questions? Given the problems of relying on self-reports, could the expert's colleagues be interviewed to validate and extend the expert's self-report?

5. Once the critical events, project reviews, or deep-smarts interviews are captured, who in the organization could present the results in a form that will be useful to successors? Which format (a text report, a summary schematic, or some other presentation) would be most useful to your group?

## Questions for Knowledge Recipients

1. Which team leader or manager have you noticed handling a critical incident or solving a complex problem particularly well?

2. How could you invite this person to share the thought processes that went into his or her decisions and skillful exercise of judgment?

# 6

# Accelerating the Transfer of Tacit Knowledge

When Jerry Winthrop joined "Balfour Paper" as a manager in corporate HR, he made a highly unusual request. He asked to work in operations for a while, so that he would understand the strong, team-based, nonunion company culture—and also learn something about the technical side of the business. He had been told about the corporate values established early on by the company founders: teamwork, treating people well, personal responsibility, honesty and integrity, a can-do attitude, and a strong work ethic. But were those really lived on a daily basis?

It was a brave undertaking for a psychology major with an MBA in organizational behavior. He had minimal mechanical aptitude and no relevant engineering skills. Moreover, the team bonuses depended on performance, so any team he joined was taking a large risk.

However, as he recalls, "the team enabled me to be successful."

Balfour was an integrated operation, meaning the colocated pulp mill provided the raw material for the paper machines, each of which was itself a huge operation turning out various paper products, from newsprint to polished paper for fine stationery. The team started him out on work that did not affect output: emptying trash cans, painting, pressure washing. Gradually, the team members taught him operational skills. First they had him observe as they monitored and repaired the rollers and reels. Next, a team member, standing by in case he was needed, would say, "You try it; it's just like what I did." Then the lead man on the crew, with a lot of know-how and years of experience, would himself take on the maintenance chores (e.g., painting) so that Jerry could learn other responsibilities like running the crane, setting up and adjusting the rollers, and checking the surface finish of the paper coming out of the calender (the roller) section.

By the end of the year, Jerry could perform many of the operational tasks that had been totally foreign to him, from operating the forklift or crane to running the presses or fixing a breakdown. (The name of the company and individual are both disguised at the request of our respondent, but the story is real.)

## Gaining Experience: Real and Vicarious

Jerry Winthrop's experience illustrates the gold standard for developing deep smarts—working alongside the experts; observing them in action; engaging in lots of practice with frequent, knowledgeable feedback; and identifying and emulating their skilled behaviors and thought patterns. In the previous two chapters, we've introduced a number of techniques and tools to facilitate the transfer of knowledge, with an emphasis on the explicit and implicit dimensions. Those techniques rely heavily on questioning, skillful facilitation, and analysis of experts' past experiences. In this chapter, we focus on experience, both real and vicarious, to capture and transfer the tacit dimensions of knowledge.

## *Accelerating Transfer through Guided Mini-Experiences*

By now, we trust we have established a basic fact about the unspoken, often unarticulated knowledge in your head. It got there through experience. Much of your tacit knowledge actually deserves that much-misused descriptor: unique. No one else has quite the same knowledge. How then can an experienced executive or subject-matter expert transfer any of that experience-based knowledge to someone lacking the same life experiences?

The answer, as we have repeatedly noted, is that not all this knowledge can be transferred. But in this chapter, we describe two methods of interaction that enable the knowledge recipient to develop some of the know-how that makes the expert so valuable. Both methods rely upon re-creating some of the expert's deep smarts, either through personal guided experience like Jerry's at Balfour or its more easily implemented cousin, discovery-based vicarious experience. Critical to both these methods is engaging the recipients' brains actively—forcing diagnosis, decision making, and problem solving about real-world situations. We start with the most valuable but also the most time-intensive mode of learning, an accelerated apprenticeship, before we turn to learning through exercises and simple simulations of experience.

While people develop pattern recognition and system thinking through experience, it would be inefficient, if not impossible, for a learner to go through the same, often lengthy experiences that have built an expert's deep smarts. However, we can design *mini-experiences* that create receptors and pattern recognition for successors or learners. Especially when such small samples of formative experiences are both selected by and guided by the experts, the learners can re-create some of the implicit and tacit smarts the organization needs to preserve and develop further.

### An Accelerated Apprenticeship Program

To help learners efficiently build their capabilities in systems perspective and pattern recognition, we have developed a structured process of guided experiences called OPPTY (for Observation, Practice, Partnering and joint problem solving, and Taking responsibilitY). Observation involves shadowing an expert and systematically analyzing what he or she does. Practice requires identifying some aspect of the expert's behavior or a specific task that the learner can do with supervision and feedback. Partnering and joint problem solving require more active participation and analytical contributions by the learner. Finally, when the learner is ready, he or she can take over a significant part of the expert's role. Along the way, the learner also deliberately reflects and receives coaching on each experience so as to internalize the knowledge as much as possible. OPPTY is applicable not only for transfers between two individuals, but also between several experts to one learner or one expert to several learners.

## OPPTY versus Traditional Mentoring

The accelerated apprenticeship program we suggest is similar to mentoring programs in many organizations, in which a senior person works with one or more junior colleagues to train them in the ways of the business and sometimes also to impart specific technical skills. However, the program we describe in this chapter differs from most such mentoring programs in several ways. First, it is structured for efficiency as well as efficacy (hence *accelerated*). Second, it is designed to help the experts impart their wisdom even more effectively and, third, it helps the learners assume a much more active role in their own progress than is traditional. Finally, and most important, the program is based on an understanding that tacit knowledge can be transferred only through experience, but that experience can be re-created very mindfully, in a tailored learning process that can be monitored and evaluated. We intend to abbreviate the mentoring, without losing the very essence of such a process—the transfer of expertise.

The *efficiency* of OPPTY comes from narrowing the focus of the transfer to the really critical parts of the experts' deep smarts and from systematically selecting mini-experiences best suited to re-creating that expertise. Transfer *efficacy* is aided when the experts understand both why tacit knowledge is so critical and how people learn. And both efficiency and efficacy are enhanced when the learners are responsible for actively identifying and eliciting the knowledge they need. Rather than passively waiting for a mantle of expertise to be draped over them, the recipients sit in the hot seat, responsible for vigorously exercising mental muscles. Therefore, the transfer process is a shared responsibility. That model of learning differs from the one emphasized from kindergarten through most graduate school education, that of a one-way flow of expertise from guru to acolyte. Even in many mentoring programs or longer apprenticeship programs, learners are not expected to actively "pull" knowledge from the more experienced person. But that expectation is prominent in OPPTY and in other similar programs (see the sidebar "Eliciting Knowledge at Baker Hughes").

# Eliciting Knowledge at Baker Hughes

At Baker Hughes, the culture is such that the responsibility for learning falls in the hands of the successor. At the mentee's initiative, he or she and the mentor first meet for one hour to brainstorm topics for knowledge transfer. A matrix is developed with topics, objectives, and resources (including people and documents) for the mentee to access. Then the two meet approximately once a month to work the plan. Although the expert provides the mini-experiences, the access for observation and practice, and the knowledgeable coaching necessary for transfer, the successor takes the initiative in developing the relationship and much of the responsibility for eliciting the knowledge.[a]

a. Wesley Vestal, HR director for Baker Hughes Integrated Operations, email to author (DL), November 18, 2013.

## An OPPTY Story

Let's look at a specific case of how OPPTY works. Jack is the vice president of international sales for the "International Mining Company" (IMC), a company selling mining equipment. Jack's sales record is legendary in IMC, and the company president has been heard to say that he'd like "ten more Jacks." In Jack's forty years of working for IMC, he has acquired an immense reservoir of experience. IMC's products represent a huge investment for mining companies—between $4 million and $12 million for a single truck or excavator. And sales go through distributors, not directly from IMC to the end user, so sales always involve a delicate dance between the demands of the dealer and those of the manufacturer he represents. Pricing is not fixed, margins are slim, and the distributor represents more than one manufacturer. Moreover, IMC customers are located around the world. It's a tough sales environment. Jack attributes his success primarily to having carefully nurtured relationships inside and outside the company, not just having an encyclopedic knowledge about the products and their virtues. He is willing to try to pass along what he knows to a successor, but he is a bit pessimistic that it's possible. How can he teach experience?

His possible successor is determined to try to make the transfer work. Steve has a BS in Civil and Environmental Engineering from Carnegie Mellon University, and he has worked overseas for a construction company. So he does have some expertise of his own. And not everything that Jack knows is equally valuable, of course. Steve doesn't intend to become a carbon copy of Jack, but he wishes he had Jack's ability to work with distributors, who are the key to all sales. Jack must also have some secret sauce for managing up, since he has worked at the same basic job even as IMC has changed ownership three times, each time with headquarters in a different country and culture. Steve needs to unearth the essential skills that have made Jack so successful—and figure out how to internalize and mimic those behaviors.

Steve knows about different ways he can learn some of these behaviors, and the methods are not mutually exclusive. He can interview Jack about his experiences and get him to tell stories that will provide vicarious experience. Steve could even use some of the question kits described in chapter 4 as a starting point. But he knows that this won't be enough. Jack is modest and tends to shrug off direct questions about his skills. "I don't do anything unusual," he says. "You'll catch on—you are smart." But Steve knows that Jack *is* unusual. And although Steve doesn't underestimate his own smarts—he knows he is a quick learner—he also knows that his learning would be accelerated if he were to be mentored by Jack. So Steve decides to approach him. When he does, Jack just smiles and agrees—but he says again, "Everything I know I got through experience. I don't think I can be much help."

That's where Jack is wrong. Experts often fail to appreciate the potential for creating the aforementioned mini-experiences in the lives of less experienced colleagues. Where did Jack get his experience? He had a summer job in construction during college, including some truck driving. He rotated through several jobs at IMC, starting at ground level in the parts department before moving to sales. He has negotiated hundreds of sales, knowing almost all the distributors on a first-name basis because he has visited them so many times. Having visited many of the mines where IMC equipment is used, Jack has heard about customer problems and delights firsthand. He has spoken at numerous mining conventions and has attended strategy meetings with IMC officials in three countries.

So the question is, How many of these experiences can he offer in miniature to Steve?

## *The OPPTY Action Plan*

In chapter 3, we discussed the importance of the contract between expert and successor, the agreement to work together to share the expert's knowledge. The initial step for setting up an OPPTY program is devising an action plan to fulfill that working contract. Most companies do something similar for their high-potential employees in the form of individualized development plans. The difference in this action plan is that OPPTY is targeted specifically at knowledge transfer, at creating expertise through *guided* experience. Of course, the nature of the expertise will determine the details. The plan for a learner working with a subject-matter expert in petroleum engineering will look quite different from one where the expert's deep smarts are in financial risk analysis. And as noted earlier, the learner bears as much responsibility to design the plan as does the expert.

There are two important parts to an action plan: setting the learning goals (along with a time frame) and designing some mini-experiences that will help the learner meet those goals. Both the expert (in this case, Jack) and probably also Jack's boss, will need to sign off on the plan.

Table 6-1 is a simplified example of what a *part* of Steve's OPPTY action plan would look like. One of Steve's long-term goals is to take over a sales region from Jack. Steve plans to reach that goal through setting intermediate goals and a time frame, and identifying a series of mini-experiences that will enable him to reach each goal. An early goal is to learn how to present IMC's products and their advantages over those of competitors, and one mini-experience will be for Steve to observe experienced sales engineers communicating with customers at an annual trade convention. After a number of such experiences, Steve moves on to his next goal, which is to begin building relationships with dealers. A mini-experience to help reach this goal is to meet with top dealers and practice the presentation skills he has been observing. With more practice, Steve wants to be able to negotiate prices, a complex process that he has observed Jack engage in expertly. Jack offers the mini-experience of joining him in negotiating a number of key deals. With many similar observations, practice sessions, and partnering with Jack over an extended time, Steve will be ready to accomplish this particular

TABLE 6-1

## Excerpts from Steve's OPPTY action plan

|  | Observation | Practice | Partnering and joint problem solving | Taking responsibility |
|---|---|---|---|---|
| Time frame goal | 2 months | 6 months | 12 months | 36 months |
|  | *Immediate goal:* Learn how to present product's competitive advantages. | *Early goal:* Start to build relationships with key dealers, and understand their position in setting prices. | *Midterm goal:* Be able to negotiate pricing with at least two dealers, on at least one product. | *Long-term goal:* Take over one sales region from Jack—one that requires more travel than Jack wants! |
| Mini-experience | Attend Jack's presentation at the annual MINExpo International; spend time at the IMC booth there, observing a more experienced sales engineer talk to customers. | Visit the top five dealers with Jack; spend a whole day alone with each of the five, talking with them and their staff and observing their operations. | Participate with Jack in negotiations with dealers on four or five key deals. Present IMC pricing position in one or more deals. | Take responsibility for selling all product lines in this geographic region. |

long-term goal. Steve's journey won't be that linear, of course, as we will explain.

Steve's ultimate overall goal is to be able to take on Jack's responsibilities, to become an autonomous, skilled manager. Table 6-1 illustrates just one of those responsibilities. The action plan contributes to this process in several ways. First, the various parts of Jack's job can be treated independently, each with its own time frame and benchmarks. If it turns out that some of these component tasks are not suitable for Steve, or if Jack decides they should be modified, eliminated, or assigned to someone else, the plan can be readily changed. Second, the OPPTY process is structured, but can be tailored to the individual. Each of the four OPPTY steps involves different levels of skill attainment, so they will normally be sequential for any one targeted capability, but the selection of actions is determined by the learner's skill level. For example, Steve might be ready to partner with Jack on some of Jack's work with distributors, but for other aspects of the job, Steve may need to start by merely observing him. Third, rather than trying to achieve a long-term goal immediately, the sequential, stepwise process acknowledges the importance of developing receptors, closing knowledge gaps gradually, and thus increasing the likelihood that the long-term goals will be achieved. Fourth, given suggested timelines and deadlines, Steve's progress can be monitored at each step, with Jack's expert feedback facilitating the transfer of knowledge. Small successes can be celebrated, goals adjusted if necessary, and failures corrected before they become serious or fatal. Finally, the more experiences that can be provided by the expert and the more often the expert can provide answers and guidance for the successor, the more effective the learning process will be. And we suggest another way of making these plans extremely meaningful: a learning log.

Steve used a learning log to track his progress (tables 6-2, 6-3, and 6-4). It's tempting to think a log is unnecessary work because we all remember very well what we've observed or done and assume we understand why experts behave as they do. But we are fooling ourselves! Moreover, the learning log is not just a recording of experiences but also a checklist of questions the learner should consider and review with the expert. The log forces both parties to examine assumptions about the mini-experiences—whether the experiences produced the desired learning. The expert may be surprised to find what the learner observed and learned (or didn't), and the learner may be able to teach the old dog a few new tricks that occurred to the less experienced (but more open-minded) learner. A learning log also serves as an accurate record of progress. And if you think it could be tedious, you might recall Thomas Edison's famous log when he was inventing the lightbulb. He made more than a thousand tries before he got it right—all recorded!

Now let's consider each of the OPPTY steps in more detail.

## Observation

Observing the expert's deep smarts in action allows a learner to begin to understand how the expert distinguishes critical signals from the noise of overwhelming data, diagnoses specific problems in the field, and adjusts to different contexts—that is, behaves differently with different customers or in different situations. In Steve's case, he first observed Jack and others presenting the product's competitively attractive features (for example, why and how an excavator can outperform a wheeled loader). Similarly, at Balfour Paper, Jerry Winthrop's first step in his technical development was observing the other team members monitoring and repairing the rollers and the reels.

Observation is surprisingly tricky. Even when the deeply smart expert's skill is obvious to the learners, they may not notice *how* the expert achieves the result. For example, consider the leader we mentioned in chapter 2, whose team members would do anything for her. They knew that Rebecca motivated their team much more than other project managers did theirs. But, they said, they didn't know *how she did it*. Then they recounted for us a number of her behaviors that would seem to explain the mystery perfectly well: she always took the blame for things that went wrong and gave credit to others when things went well. On trips to clients, she took team members along and gave them the chance to make part of the presentations. She matched assignments to team members' interests and gave them extra opportunities to learn. And when they made mistakes, she told them about her own screw-ups. Who wouldn't want to work for her? So why didn't they see the connection between these behaviors and what they wanted to learn from her? Their observations were not conscious until we probed for them. Smart as they were, these team members never set up a deliberate plan for learning one of the skills they valued the most. So they didn't learn it.

Conscious observation can also prove challenging because sometimes the learner is both absorbing some new content—new information about the domain—and at the same time trying to notice the expert's behavior. That is, the learner must focus not only on what is being said or done but also on how those actions contribute to the desired result. Writing down both content and process in the learning log helps the learner reflect on the experience and identify the behaviors and skills of the expert. Time for reflection is critical to learning. For another example of conscious observation, see the sidebar "Observation at Microsoft."

During observation, a learner can note, for example:

- The context: where, who was involved, and what was the expert's purpose or goal?

- What the expert did—and why.

- The apparent results of those actions.

After the fact, the learner can ask the expert questions such as these:

- Why did you do X?

- How did you know how to do Y?

- What did you expect would happen?

Reflecting on the observation, the learner can think about issues such as the following:

- What worked and what didn't?

- Were the effects on others beneficial or not?

Table 6-2 provides some excerpts from Steve's observation learning log.

TABLE 6-2

## Excerpts from Steve's learning log: observation

|  | Steve's notes | Observations | Reflections |
| --- | --- | --- | --- |
| Context | MINExpo International. | I noticed multiple booths; KSF much larger than ours; better brochures. | Competitors' collateral materials better quality than ours—why? |
| Expert's actions | Jack gave hour-long presentation: slides, video, and took questions from floor. | Good presentation skills; he is very enthusiastic about our products and mining; video was dramatic. | The audience really perked up when he showed the video; quotes from satisfied customers good idea. How did he choose those? Seems like an idea I could apply in the future to a lot of situations. |

# Observation at Microsoft

Chris Capossela, executive vice president and chief marketing officer at Microsoft, recalls a valuable learning experience he had as a young employee. Six years after joining Microsoft right out of college, Capossela was hired to work as a speech assistant to Bill Gates. While Capossela did his share of grunt work (hotel check-ins, ordering food), he also had some heady experiences, such as sitting in on meetings with other top executives in the industry. "The time I got to spend with Bill as his speech assistant gave me exposure to so many things I would never have otherwise seen. From observing Bill in action, I learned to always stay curious and open to new information and to never miss an opportunity to teach more junior team members." One of the things he observed was that Gates used every meeting to achieve a particular goal, sometimes promoting Microsoft and sometimes negotiating a new partnership. Gates also thought very strategically about conduct during meetings, for example, about the advantages of not being the first to speak in negotiations. Capossela was able to ask Gates questions after the meetings about why he chose to behave in certain ways and how he made decisions on the fly. And after each trip, Capossela wrote up a trip report. The postmeeting debrief with Gates and the trip report were essential steps in internalizing lessons that he had learned.[a]

a. Chris Capossela, interview with author (GB), November 18, 2013.

## *Practice*

As we discussed, deliberate practice with expert feedback is fundamental to the development of any type of expertise. The value of a structured mentorship is that it provides a continuous loop of practice opportunities, time for reflection, and internalization using the learning logs, with feedback from knowledgeable mentors. The practice/reflection/learning feedback loop stimulates the learning by the successor and speeds up the knowledge-transfer process, which might otherwise take much longer. For Balfour Paper's Jerry Winthrop, the guided practice he experienced in operations helped develop not only the organizational cultural knowledge he originally sought about teamwork, honesty, integrity, and personal responsibility, but also his technical and physical skills.

Some generic examples of opportunities to practice with mentor feedback might include the preparation and presentation of part of a report to upper management or customers, leading a portion of a meeting, or gathering data on a geographic region. With the support of the expert, the successor can test his or her own growing know-how by initially diagnosing a problem before the expert does or analyzing data and comparing results with the expert's analysis of the same data. (As discussed later in this chapter, the more active are learners' brains, the more likely they will retain the lessons.) And as in the case of observation, the learner needs both to consider what questions to ask the expert and also to think about what could be done differently in the future.

One of the important benefits of practice is the opportunity to observe and assess your successes and failures and, through practice, correct those failures. For example, each time the expert Jack challenges Steve to solve a problem or take the lead in an interaction with a distributor and he successfully completes a task, it not only helps Steve internalize the behaviors but also builds his confidence in his own abilities to successfully manage the situation. More than likely, Steve will not perform everything correctly, which is why he is learning from Jack. But by also using his learning log to check progress and by checking his analysis with Jack, he begins to develop his own diagnostic and problem-solving capabilities.

After practice, the learner can record in the learning log (besides the context) the answers to questions such as these:

- What did I do, and did it work? Did it help me toward the next goal?

- What feedback did I get? Was I prepared?

- What did I learn?

Table 6-3 gives some examples from Steve's learning log.

**TABLE 6-3**

### Excerpts from Steve's learning log: practice

| | Notes on the facts | Observation lessons | Reflections |
|---|---|---|---|
| **Context** | Top three dealers. | Dealers vary a lot in their emphasis on price, quality, service. | Good icebreaker to talk about families—but need to know first if the guy is still married. (Big *oops* with Antoine.) |
| **Mini-experiences** | Went with Jack on visit; spent whole day at three dealers; visited two service departments. Went to dinner with two of them by myself. | Tony's service bay was a mess; I wouldn't send my trucks there for repairs if I were a customer. Dinner: a good place to build friendship. Hit it off well with Ken; he likes the same sports teams. | I think I'm pretty good if the dealer likes our products, but need to get better at responding when they don't. Wish I'd asked Jack more about the dealers' personal backgrounds before we went. |
| **Feedback from expert** | Talked with Jack on the way back in the car from first visit; three-day delay after the next. | Need to debrief with Jack right after I practice something; he doesn't remember well after a delay. | Jack says I need to learn to like beer. Was he kidding or serious? He said I have good "contact" skills—what does that mean? |

## Partnering and Joint Problem Solving

As the successor or successors move forward in the OPPTY process, there will be opportunities to work with the expert to solve problems. In some cases, the two may have already worked together and combined expertise on projects, but new opportunities for joint work can be specifically designed to transfer knowledge.

During partnering and joint problem solving, learners ask many of the same questions and record in the learning log much as before:

- What was the problem or situation?

- What did we do to address it?

- What worked? What didn't work?

- Where do the expert and I see differently?

- Can I suggest some adjustments to the process?

Joint problem solving can introduce the learners not only to the problems, but also to colleagues who have specialized knowledge that might be usefully applied to future problems. For example, consider the wisdom of a defense contractor senior engineer when he took his mentee to the end of the missile assembly line to work collaboratively with a technician conducting final testing. It was highly unusual for a design engineer to leave the rarefied air of his department and descend to the lowly assembly floor. But the senior engineer wanted to help his mentee develop design know-how and system thinking. Design flaws and dysfunctional component interactions showed up only at the final test, because up to that point, component parts had been tested separately or in subsets. The experience helped the mentee understand how the entire missile system worked and what problems might occur between the initial design and the final assembly. It also disabused her of the notion that engineering design had the only smarts in the organization—and incidentally, introduced her to a very experienced technician whose advice she might need sometime.

As successors approach equality with the expert, they can contribute their own perspectives and capabilities as they pair up to identify, diagnose, and solve problems. In some instances, the successor may request or be assigned responsibility for acquiring knowledge or skills not possessed by the expert, but needed by the organization (e.g., entering the Chinese market) and sharing those with the expert. In other cases, during joint work, the introduction of the successor's perspective may lead to emerging knowledge and innovation. For example, as we will describe in chapter 9, a newly hired PhD at Alcoa found, after conducting statistical analysis, a way to greatly increase productivity by focusing on the performance of individual furnaces instead of making adjustments based on the average performance of all of the furnaces.

In some cases, the combination of the expert's knowledge and the different perspectives of the successor may lead to innovation. In the excerpts from Steve's learning log (table 6-4), note the increasing sophistication of Steve's observations and reflections compared to his observation and practice learning logs.

## *Taking Responsibility*

If the joint problem solving goes well, the successor is now ready to take responsibility for part or all of the role of the expert. In Steve's case, he won the right to manage sales in a given region. He achieved one of his original long-term goals.

Steve hasn't stopped learning, of course, and he may find it very useful to continue with the learning log as a powerful help in self-reflection. Nor has he become Jack's clone. What Steve has accomplished, through multiple mini-experiences, is to absorb some of the tacit knowledge Jack accrued over so many years of service. The world of mining equipment is changing no less than that of other industries. Products evolve. But sales are sales are sales. What Steve has learned about interacting with distributors and customers will remain valuable in the future, even if the equipment becomes more robotic.

TABLE 6-4

## Excerpts from Steve's learning log: partnering and joint problem solving

|  | Notes on the facts | Observation lessons | Reflections |
|---|---|---|---|
| **Context** | Negotiations with Ken Dodge, dealer. | Ken is really hurting in this economy. But having our warranties helps the dealers like him a lot. | I think we could keep a bit higher margins on the excavators; we have a real advantage there. |
| **Mini-experiences** | Jack and I discussed pricing before we went in. Decided on a "walk-away" price. Discussed with Ken what information he needed, when, for big potential sale. | Jack is inclined to give dealers the best possible discount, because without them, we are "dead in the water." Jack is very straightforward in his negotiations— fair but tough. | These dealers really trust Jack to do what he says, when he says he will. I might not have agreed to Ken's deadline for delivery of the marketing materials—and that would have been a mistake. |
| **Feedback from expert** | Jack said it was fun working together on this. Said he liked the way I analyzed Ken's margins. | Jack and I started out with really different prices in mind. He knows exactly how far he can discount on every product. | I think we were good partners on this deal. I know more than he does about the new technology in the products; he knows more about pricing—and his relationships are phenomenal. |

In our example, Steve and Jack were colocated. Of course, that's a great advantage in applying OPPTY. Moreover, they had time to work together. Time is definitely necessary for this process—but given the rich media of today, colocation is not an absolute requirement. Moreover, OPPTY is not restricted to a one-to-one arrangement. A learner can learn from several experts, and certainly an expert can guide the experience of more than one learner. The acquisition of deep smarts is a lifelong pursuit. Every job transition offers the chance to apply the principles of OPPTY.

Taking responsibility for the expert's role is the culmination of the OPPTY process. However, in a more general sense, there is much that the learner can do to take responsibility for his or her own learning throughout an OPPTY-like process, even in the absence of a formal program. Perhaps the organization is not prepared to set up such structured accelerated apprenticeships. In that case, people like Steve can take the initiative, supported by managers who can encourage them to be more proactive on their own behalf. Learners can construct their own knowledge development plan, identifying possible gaps in their training that they might want to fill or picking possible experiences that might be useful to their career development. They might have to actively lobby to attend a meeting, visit a customer, or help solve a problem. If they are currently doing joint work with an expert, they could be more deliberate in observing how the expert diagnoses a problem or leads a team meeting. By taking a few moments after each experience to note the actions of the expert, reflecting on how their own processes can be improved, and identifying lessons learned in their work, learners can go a long way toward building their own expertise. And if possible, they should find some time with experts to ask for feedback on their observations, their practicing, and their problem solving.

## The Art of Knowledge Transfer through Discovery

A fully realized OPPTY initiative, which we consider the gold standard for transferring tacit knowledge, requires substantial resources—financial, time, personnel. The need for expertise to be passed on, and the costs of not doing so, must be recognized. Most organizations do not have knowledge transfer built into their operations. Instead, they need to make special efforts to transfer know-how. (In our survey of CIOs, CTOs, and HR executives, only 23 percent indicated that their organization had a specific program dedicated to knowledge transfer.) In the face of a lack of resources, your temptation will likely be to resort to lectures by the experts to the learners as the most expeditious mode of transfer. You know that you can't possibly re-create expert decision-making and diagnostic capabilities in learners' minds that way. Yet those deep smarts are what your organization truly needs. Fortunately, recognizing that a key component of the OPPTY process is allowing the learner to actively discover the knowledge allows us to suggest some alternative strategies.

## Beyond Lectures

Please humor us by taking a moment to consider a riddle:

*The keys were useless because the air was gone.*

Huh? Try to make sense of this statement before reading further. Struggle with it. Entertain hypotheses. If that was too easy (or too hard), try to figure out this one:

*The haystack was important because the cloth ripped.*

Our guess is that eventually you will discover that "accordion" provides the context to make sense of the first sentence, and "parachute" will generate the appropriate "aha!" reaction to the second. We also think that you are likely to remember these little examples better than other parts of this chapter, despite our deathless prose, because you had to actively exercise your brain to try to understand them. If individuals wrestle with a problem before discovering a solution, the experience stays in long-term memory much better than if they have been simply told the answer.[1]

Active involvement in your own learning has long been recognized as more effective than a more passive, spoon-fed approach (see the sidebar "Working the Brain Harder Makes Learning Easier"). Simulations such as role-playing scenarios and case studies that require reflection and analysis prior to your arriving at a decision can be close approximations to the challenges faced in the real world.

# Working the Brain Harder
# Makes Learning Easier

We often deceive ourselves when we think we've learned some-thing. And the easier it was to access the information, the more confident we are in our learning. Fooled again! Psychologists—and teachers—have long known that our beliefs about how well we've learned a subject are way off. And when we use crutches such as answers provided in the back of the book (or a click away in an online course)—we are apt to think we've got those problems nailed. But research has shown the fallacy of that assumption. Experiments with different levels of exposure to problem solutions—including some that were so disguised that the participants didn't even realize they'd previously seen the answers—show that such "help" only increases confidence, not performance.[a] It turns out that we tend to confuse ease of *storing* information with the ease of *retrieving* it. Easy *in* does not equate to easy *out*. In fact, quite the opposite is true: the harder it is to process information, the easier it is to access it when we need it. This effect has been demonstrated in experiments such as ones that require the participants to create a sensible outline out of a flawed one or having to read material in an unfamiliar font. It may seem counterintuitive that working harder is actually more effi-cient, but greater effort and better concentration lead to deeper and more lasting learning. What does that say about trying to transfer knowledge through lectures? Or online courses that pro-vide solutions along with the problem?

a. Benedict Carey, "Come On, I Thought I Knew That!" *New York Times*, April 19, 2011, D5–D6.

## An Example of Discovery in Action

The US Army's Leader Challenge embodies active discovery in the classroom. An experienced military leader (usually through video, but sometimes in person) poses a dilemma that he or she has personally experienced in the field. Here's an example: in Iraq, the US platoon leader has been on an extended patrol and is returning to base when an improvised explosive device (IED) kills one of his soldiers. After personally carrying the dead soldier to the MEDEVAC helicopter, he receives an order from the company commander. The leader presents the challenge he faced to a class as follows:

> *Coming back from an all-night foot patrol, Sgt. H. was hit by an IED. He didn't make it. After getting him MEDEVAC'd out, I began thinking about what I was going to tell the platoon once we got back to our base. Then, the commander called and gave me a direct order to clear the nearest village, where the guys who put in the IED could be located—a mission that would easily take eight hours. My guys were out of food and water, were already physically smoked, and they were pissed off about Sgt. H. He was easily the men's favorite team leader, and there's no way those people [Iraqis] didn't know something about that IED. Then my trusted platoon sergeant tells me, "Sir, there is no way we can do this mission. Look at the guys!" At that point, my company commander called again to find out why I wasn't moving to the village. What do I do?*[2]

The classroom of learners now has the opportunity to discuss what to do, including thinking through potential second-order effects, both in the moment and long term. After exploring the possibilities and potential consequences of each action, the participants watch the second part of the video, which reveals what the platoon leader did. He occupied a building in the village where he took a tactical pause to refit with water and to explain to his men what happened and what their new mission was. The platoon then conducted the mission and returned to base.

The objective of having the learners actively grapple with a complex issue such as this one before being told how it was resolved is to instill judgment (recall that wise decision making is a hallmark of deep smarts). Learners are warned that the solution reached in a particular case was not the only possible solution—perhaps not even the best. There is no way that the soldiers can be prepared for all contingencies by remembering specific solutions. But these learners will have to make such decisions quickly, using the best information available at the time; the Leader Challenge is a kind of simulation of the real world in which the soldiers will lead. Feedback from participants included such statements as: "This *works*. How do I get more of these Challenges?"[3] Not only did the challenges build confidence in decision making, but the exercise also helped the learners figure out what they didn't know and where they had been overconfident.

Discovery exercises similar to the army's are deployed effectively in business settings as well. Using vignettes for training has produced a statistically significant improvement in situation awareness, sense making, and planning skills.[4] For example, Holly Baxter recounts a technique that begins with a subject-matter expert preparing a scenario of a situation that required a decision. The background and other relevant information were provided, but not the action taken by the subject-matter expert. The scenario was presented to the knowledge recipients, who shared with one another their thoughts, including the pros and cons of various possible decisions. Only then was the actual decision taken by the expert presented. Baxter describes this method as "a simple technique that puts students in the moment and gives surrogate experience, which enhances knowledge transfer."[5]

Simulations in the hands of individuals who have no real-world experience can lead to miscalculations. Product designers report saving lots of money avoiding the necessity of building physical prototypes by using simulations. At the same time, though, says Ashlee Vance, some critics see drawbacks in simulations:

> *Design experts say they worry that young engineers now place too much emphasis on simulation and not enough on knowing how to build physical objects. Ultimately, it's an engineer who establishes the constraints of the software, and setting the simulation parameters requires awareness of the physical world's complexities. "[Practice with simulations] won't make a bad engineer good," says Jim Cashman III, CEO of Ansys, the largest producer of simulation software. "It will make a good engineer great."* [6]

And that's what we are after—experience building that creates deep smarts. Computerized simulations employed to train airplane pilots or doctors in medical school build tacit knowledge through repeated, highly realistic experiences. Be thankful that the pilot on your next flight and the surgeon who replaces your knee, hip, or heart had experience with simulations. Such simulations allow the user to accumulate vicarious experiences, from which learners will derive principles of decision making and behavior and will develop the sensory skills that help build their expertise.

Software-based simulations are expensive to build and are not a likely option for transferring the deep smarts of a particular individual or group in your organization. However, discovery exercises like the US Army's Leader Challenge are well within your reach, given the ease of video creation. We know of a worldwide construction company whose managers puzzled over how to transfer the expertise of their troubleshooters without constantly flying these experts around the world. One solution the managers came up with was to videotape common construction problems, such as water damage from inadequate preparation of walls. The YouTube-like video did not have high production value, but the stains and crumbling stucco from the problem were clearly visible. After some context was provided (climate, age), workers in far-flung regions of the company were asked to view the video, diagnose what had happened, and suggest a remedy. Only then was the cause explained and the preventative steps demonstrated, again by video.

Similarly, in your company you can create short text vignettes of dilemmas specific to your operations. The critical-incident technique we described in chapter 5 is also a form of simulation, although it does not have the element of discovery unless you take the story in pieces, asking at various points what those unfamiliar with the details might have done, what information they might have sought, or whom they would have contacted. If you do so, the critical incident begins to approximate the cases that are used as text simulations in so many business school classrooms around the world.

Simulations, guided experience, and discovery exercises all have the same objectives. First, they all build, through repeated decision making, a repertoire of experiences and associated patterns on which learners can draw when considering possible responses. Second, these techniques all create a relatively safe environment in which to fail forward—that is, to learn from making wrong decisions without penalty to the learners themselves or others. Failure is highly memorable, so these experiences are a low-cost way to imprint system thinking, that is, to learn to anticipate possible implications of an action on others' subsequent decisions and actions. Third, these techniques all create a sense of self-efficacy in the learners, enhanced confidence in their ability to address future situations and problems. The effectiveness of all these methods is best determined by the ability of the learners to demonstrate expertise in the real world. The usual separation in time and situation between the learning process and its eventual outcome makes evaluation difficult—but not impossible. In the next chapter, we describe various ways that organizations can assess the success of knowledge transfer, including the transfer techniques we have described.

## Questions for Managers

1.  What responsibilities do current experts have that could be eventually assumed by learners?

2.  What learners in your organization would most benefit from an OPPTY action plan?

3.  What kinds of mini-experiences can be created for such learners? Can you think of some specific opportunities for observation, practice, and partnering?

4.  How could some learning goals be clearly elucidated for such learners?

5.  How could you make OPPTY work when experts and learners are geographically distant from each other?

6.  How will you ensure conscientious follow-through on the OPPTY action plans? How could you obtain an agreement between experts and learners for frequent checkpoints to assess progress?

7.  Which current training processes for learners throughout your organization could be converted into discovery exercises? Could vignettes of typical, but specific dilemmas faced by the experts be created as (noncomputerized) simulations?

## Questions for Knowledge Recipients

1.  How would you develop your own OPPTY action plan? What mini-experiences would you like to have?

2.  How could you set up a learning log to record your observations of experts' actions that seem particularly effective and worth emulating?

# 7

# Assessing the Transfer
# of Deep Smarts

How do we know if our learners have deepened their smarts? Wouldn't it be great if we could peer into their brains before and after our attempts to transfer knowledge and see whether there's a greater accumulation of decision-making ability, more mental patterns based on experience, and perhaps more emotional intelligence? But even the most sophisticated PET or fMRI imaging technology that illuminates and isolates brain activity can't tell us that yet. Measuring the success of knowledge transfer is, like evaluating any other exchange among humans, tricky!

Sometimes the loss of critical expertise is so likely in an organization, and the potential loss so imminent and so dangerous, that preserving the knowledge is a strategic imperative. Attempts to precisely assess the impact of the loss or to justify the transfer program on the basis of financial return would be an exercise in creativity but largely beside the point. The assumption is that doing nothing about certain losses will almost certainly be costly, and therefore any effort that yields perceived benefits, no matter how hard it is to quantify them, is justified. As one CIO said to us of the expense involved in having an expert mentor a successor, "if he learns even ten to fifteen percent of what that expert knows, the effort will be worthwhile." Let's look at an example of a project to safeguard knowledge that meets both these strategic criteria: critical knowledge loss at stake, under severe time pressure.

In chapter 4 we described knowledge transfer during a pharmaceutical company's acquisition of a competitor. Consultants trained the acquiring organization's scientists and researchers to transfer knowledge about the drug development programs under way at the acquired corporation. There was no formal assessment of the success of the knowledge transfer—any such effort would have taken valuable time away from the transfer program itself. Nonetheless, the deep dive into the knowledge in the acquisition yielded the desired benefits: the merger met the targets laid out for creating synergy, on time and within budget. But even more important in the long term was a critical decision directly attributable to the knowledge-transfer project. The acquiring company ("LPC") had planned to lay off a number of researchers in the acquisition. However, during the knowledge-transfer process, scientists in LPC uncovered unrivaled skills for drug discovery among those candidates for layoff—better, in fact, than their own. These deeply smart individuals were left in place to continue work that ultimately greatly benefited LPC. That talent (and the tacit knowledge in the scientists' heads) would have migrated to other competitors had it not been retained.

Not all knowledge-loss situations cry out "strategic necessity" as did this example. As we saw in chapter 1, managers can be keenly aware that there will be costs, but unless these costs are painful as well as immediate, it may be difficult to convince decision makers that a knowledge-transfer program is truly necessary. Ideally, the manager should be able to build a strong business case, along with an assessment methodology that will demonstrate the effectiveness of the transfer. There is no single best way to evaluate the success of a transfer process, but we will give you an overview of several promising ones, categorized according to two models of knowledge sharing.

# Assessment in Two Models of Knowledge Transfer

Assessment of success obviously depends on what we were intending to accomplish. (Fun journey, but did we end up in the right city?) The examples of knowledge transfer we've given you throughout the book fall roughly into two basic approaches. The first is sharing through networks, usually electronically (e.g., in communities of practice), where knowledge flows among people who may or may not know each other. While individual learners in such systems certainly do increase their knowledge base, the emphasis is on solving problems in real time, archiving information for future access, and raising the smarts of the entire network. The second approach is more focused on raising the competency of selected learners through interviews and work with subject-matter experts or experienced executives. These two approaches are by no means mutually exclusive. Some networks include mentoring, and some programs aimed at raising individual competency also tie into centers of excellence or other kinds of networks. But for simplicity's sake, we'll talk about assessments in the two separately as network-capability based and individual- or group-competency based (table 7-1).

In both these models, you can measure *input* in terms of investment of effort or time to set up and monitor the network (in the first model) or to create and carry out the knowledge-sharing program (in the second). As we saw earlier with strategically critical programs, we may take on faith that such inputs yield value—to the organization or the individuals involved. It is not unreasonable to assume that if an educational program was well designed and delivered, then valuable learning probably occurred.

However, everyone would prefer to assess success in terms of *output*—whether there is an observable change in the level or quality of knowledge. (The proof, as the saying goes, is in the pudding—not

TABLE 7-1

## Assessing knowledge-transfer success

| | Network-capability based | Individual- or group-competency based |
| --- | --- | --- |
| Input (effort; investment) | Infrastructure for knowledge sharing; creation of networks; tracking of participation; leadership of communities | Investment of time and effort in workshops and knowledge-sharing sessions; mentoring; being mentored |
| Output (changed state) | Increase in archives of knowledge tips; answers to inquiries; increased participation in networks | Achieving greater competence; narrowing gap between experts and learners, incumbents and successors |
| Value to organization | Swift solution of problems; global access to expertise; high level of connectivity; diffusion of best practices | Less relearning; fewer mistakes; better job performance; better succession planning |
| Measures of value | Cost avoidance; testimonials of value received | Gap closure; learning log; achieving competency level; recognition as expert; promotion |

in the ingredients or the effort.) Then the next question is, does that changed state have value? And if we think so, how do we measure the value? In the world of business, the term *value* tends to have dollar signs attached. But there are other ways of measuring success.

Since the operation and objectives of these two kinds of knowledge-transfer systems differ, so do the assessments to measure their effectiveness. In the first model, we often measure success by quantifying the growth and use of the network, the assumption being that if more people are using it, and are using it more frequently, then the network must be effective. Other criteria are the speed and utility of responses to inquiries. Useful new knowledge can be archived for retrieval, often through highly structured, automated processes. Most of the knowledge to be transferred is implicit (not captured and often not previously voiced) or already explicit—but not really tacit.

# Network Capability Model

Suppose you are a manager in ConocoPhillips, a company that has made huge investments in software systems that span its often far-flung operations and allow the identification of experts, dialogue, questions, and responses. How can you justify the expense? Luckily, one of the great advantages of such systems is their ability to auto-matically record interactions and spit out numbers about usage—essentially the "aggregating eyeballs" evidence of output.

ConocoPhillips has been awarded the annual Most Admired Knowledge Enterprise (MAKE) award for which organizations are nominated and elected by a large number of academics and profes-sionals working in knowledge management. One reason for so honor-ing ConocoPhillips is the company's very visible and well-documented Networks of Excellence (NoEs). An internal system tracks increases in portal hits for the NoEs. So, for example, between 2008 and 2012, those searches increased dramatically from just under 800,000 to 2.25 million. Similarly, the company could report an increase in net-work membership from 777 in 2005 to just under 15,000 in 2011, with many employees belonging to more than one network—on aver-age, 2.8 per person in 2010.[1]

## *Cost Avoidance*

So you can document increases in membership and portal hits. Those numbers undeniably show an increase in traffic—evidence of a growing community. But what about the value of all that activity? Like most other companies that utilize communities of practice to share knowledge, ConocoPhillips collected success stories, which were often tales of cost savings. As the NoEs became increasingly an accepted part of routine work, these stories became less impor-tant metrics of success. But at their height in 2008, there were over fifteen hundred such testimonials of value. Many stories recounted how a specific individual saved time and effort by locating the solution to a particular problem. For example, a question originated in Indonesia: Was it safe to extend the run time of a power turbine beyond its scheduled overhaul period? Members of the Upstream Rotating Equipment NoE responded that extending the time was indeed safe—a solution that avoided an unnecessary expenditure and allowed rescheduling the shutdown for maintenance to a better time.[2] Similarly, a Well-Optimization NoE set cost-avoidance goals for itself and succeeded in reducing unplanned losses due to equipment problems by 10 percent a year.[3]

## Diffusing Best Practices

Other benefits delivered from network-based knowledge sharing accrue from identifying a best practice in one business or geographic location and subsequently spreading the practice to other locations around the world. ConocoPhillips discovered in its Australian operations a new technique for conducting underwater ballast tank inspections using remotely operated vehicles. This practice was not only utilized in the company's own North Sea operations but was picked up by others in the industry.[4] While it is not always possible to assign a dollar value to the adoption of such best practices, they are called "best" for a reason. Underwater robots obviously have fewer safety issues than do human divers.

## Time Savings

Yet another justification for the capital expenditures involved in setting up information-based systems is the speed with which problems are solved—a savings in labor time that results in clear cost savings. For example, when knowledge strategist Jeff Stemke was at Chevron, he built metrics into networks to measure the results of the question-and-answer process. The global refining network of two thousand engineers and operators routinely sought and received answers to questions on technical process or equipment problems that were holding up production. Asked to estimate the time and cost saved by responses from their colleagues, network users reported cost savings of over $100 million over seven years.[5] Presumably, the recipients of the solutions also experienced a concomitant rise in competence.

As you can see, even in the computer-based network model, measuring the output of knowledge transfer depends on self-report, anecdotal evidence, and gross cost-savings estimates to prove value. Our accountants may be disappointed, but unassailable, objective numbers are hard to come by. And objective measurements are similarly difficult to make when we look at the competencies-based programs.

## Assessing Knowledge Transfer in Individuals

In this second model, where the knowledge is more implicit or tacit, the process of knowledge sharing can be immediately evaluated, but the impact may not be felt for many months, delaying the assessment of its success. Moreover, the most useful archives in the competency model are usually individual rather than collective, and the players involved determine what to record and archive. Of course, when deeply smart individuals' implicit and tacit knowledge is rendered explicit, it can be shared with more than the initially designated learners or successors. In those cases, the knowledge captured can be deliberately edited and packaged for distribution or posting online in some fashion, perhaps as best practices that can be diffused to multiple successors.

In evaluating knowledge accrual among learners, some organizations describe desired competencies and then measure progress toward those goals. In essence, this is an attempt to see if learners are closing an initial gap between their starting point and the abilities of an expert. For example, the US Army, whose new recruits often come with few applicable skills, must have some way of determining if an individual is capable of learning to follow orders and then eventually grow into a capacity to lead. Think about the extraordinary expectations of young majors today in war zones. They have to be warriors, negotiators, culturally sensitive social workers, and construction supervisors! In one method of evaluating recruits, the army based its work on Hubert Dreyfus and Stuart Dreyfus's model of cognitive skill acquisition, which has five levels of proficiency, from novice to expert.[6] The military focuses on four generic requirements of the job: (1) to know and use assets; (2) to focus on mission and higher-ups' intent (i.e., what the generals want); (3) to model a "thinking enemy"; and (4) to consider the effects of the terrain.[7] The cognitive skills expected at each level are laid out quite specifically, and training is aimed at enabling learners to work their way up to each in succession. Attainment of a given level is assessed by three performance indictors: (1) responses to a verbal protocol, (2) written responses to questions, and (3) observations. The sidebar "Levels of Expertise in the US Army" provides some examples of these levels of expertise.

The army's description of the expert level in the sidebar overlaps our models of deep smarts significantly—not surprising, since our initial categorization was based on some of the same research on expertise. According to the army definition, an expert is, for example, expected to make fine distinctions, rely heavily and successfully on mental simulation to predict events, and detect problems and spot anomalies early. Sound familiar?

Many businesses use competency models somewhat similar to the army's, positing certain skills that should be reached before individuals in a particular role can be judged to have developed proficiency in that role. Competency is not the same as expertise, of course. But the measurement principle is the same: determining the closure of a gap between a novice and someone with much more experience and ability.

For example, starting in 2005, Schlumberger Business Consulting conducted an annual survey of client companies, asking how

# Levels of Expertise in the US Army

The US Army recognizes the need to develop expertise in four areas, including the ability to consider the effects of terrain. Following are the descriptors of skill attainment at three of the five levels:

**Level 1 (Novice): Uses terrain checklists.** Performance focuses on identifying discrete features of terrain. Individual uses standard checklists to determine relevant terrain features. The foundational knowledge required to analyze the impact of terrain on the mission has not yet been developed.

. . .

**Level 3 (Journeyman): Incorporates terrain into own plan.** Performance reflects a mental model of impact of terrain on the mission. Individual performs an analysis of the terrain and incorporates terrain features into the plan. For example, in an urban setting the tallest and sturdiest buildings are perceived as good locations to occupy. However, the individual tends to adhere to the plan even after the situation has evolved and new information about the terrain becomes available.

. . .

**Level 5 (Expert): Turns terrain to own advantage.** Performance reflects an ability to recognize, assess and decide. Individual is quickly able to visualize how terrain will impact the friendly mission and predicted enemy actions. He leverages the terrain to his own advantage and denies the enemy's ability to do the same.[a]

a. Jennifer K. Phillips, Karol G. Ross, and Scott B. Shadrick, "User's Guide for Tactical Thinking, Behaviorally Anchored Rating Scales," Armored Forces Research Unit, United States Army Research Institute for the Behavioral and Social Sciences, 2006, 14.

long it took for new petroleum engineers to reach a level of autonomy, defined as a certain set of individual skills the company considered relatively standard across the industry (table 7-2).

The studies found that the engineers in the companies that had mentoring and job rotation programs reach proficiency level 3 ("skill," which defined autonomy) more quickly than those that did not have these programs. In 2007, for example, the time difference in reaching level 3 was about six years. As Schlumberger Business Consulting continued the annual survey, including collecting actual job descriptions and company-generated explanations of what the companies considered requirements for autonomy, the consultants discovered that companies differed considerably in the complexity of tasks required of engineers. At some companies, the job requirements for autonomy (level 3) were more like other companies' requirements for level 4; still other companies' requirements for autonomy were more like others' level 2 requirements. So even

TABLE 7-2

## Schlumberger Business Consulting's competency requirements for petroleum engineers

| 1. Awareness | 2. Knowledge | 3. Skill | 4. Advanced | 5. Expert |
|---|---|---|---|---|
| • Recognizes or identifies technology<br>• Describes technology purpose<br>• Asks for help on technology | • Understands technology<br>• Identifies or classifies information or technology with wide criteria<br>• Generates simple products or answers<br>• Applies technology under supervision | • Applies technology independently and correctly<br>• Analyzes work processes and solves problems<br>• Diagnoses and routinely recommends solutions<br>• Supports business objectives | • Diagnoses or solves complex problems<br>• Anticipates technology impact on business<br>• Brings alternative solutions<br>• Implements technology strategy | • Generates innovative solutions, products, or both<br>• Defines new practices<br>• Establishes technology strategy<br>• Is considered company or industry authority |

*Source*: Copyright Schlumberger Oil & Gas HR Benchmark 2012; used with permission.

*Note*: The technical autonomy assessment is based on the main requirements given by the company in terms of competencies needed to reach autonomy.

defining a level of competency according to a specified set of skills is necessarily imprecise. Much depends on the organization's specific operations: when those operations are more complex, the tasks required of their engineers are more difficult and will take more time to master.

As the Schlumberger example suggests, judging a particular individual's growth in proficiency is complicated. The skills associated with each level of proficiency are generic in order to be applicable to a wide variety of individuals in the same role. Thus there are at least three limitations in using such generic models to assess progress toward expertise. First, individuals in the same role as described by the organization may in fact operate within local systems that vary in the complexity of the tasks assigned to the role. Second, individuals bring different receptors and native abilities to the role. And finally, even such structured attempts to judge skill levels depend on the subjective judgments of *someone*. The judges themselves vary both in their proximity to the assessed work, in their objectivity and biases, and in their own assessment skills. However, these role-competency models used by the army and Schlumberger can certainly help in plotting career trajectories. The individual knows in general what skills to aim for. Moreover, the organization has defined the capabilities that it needs. And there are standards against which an individual's accretion of knowledge can be measured.

How about the progress of an individual in a special knowledge-transfer program? This should be easier to evaluate, right? After all, it's just one person in a structured program. But it depends on the type of assessment employed. Success of knowledge-transfer programs is generally measured in at least one of three ways: (1) the participants' self-reported satisfaction with the program (relatively easy); (2) the participants' self-documented progress in learning, such as through a learning log (tougher); and (3) whether an initial knowledge gap between expert and learner has narrowed over time (a much rarer assessment and tougher yet—but the closest to a direct measure of value delivered).

## *Participant Satisfaction*

We all know that attendance at workshops or transfer sessions does not guarantee comprehension, much less internalization, of concepts or—the holy grail of education—demonstrated greater competence. But we can determine how worthwhile the participants considered a particular knowledge-sharing workshop or session. Strategic Knowledge Solutions consultant Holly Baxter recounts the example of feedback from a participant in a knowledge-transfer workshop. He had been working side by side with a risk management specialist who had forty years' experience to his thirty. Given their almost equivalent seniority and their joint work experience, no one expected much knowledge to be transferred. But the critical-incident review of a particular situation in which a tool had injured someone included all the steps undertaken to manage the aftermath, including public relations and fears arising from this very odd occurrence—none of which was known to the junior manager. Afterward, he wrote Holly that he was "surprised at how much new info I got from the session from someone I've talked to almost every day for five years."[8]

Anecdotes such as these are quite common, and they do evidence value delivered. Most of us don't spend a lot of time on the job thinking about actively learning from those around us or about imparting wisdom. So being given the time and the techniques to extract knowledge and internalize it can be a deeply satisfying experience. In a typical knowledge-elicitation session with a group of people, each individual learns something slightly different, filling slightly different gaps in his or her knowledge. (For more commentary on knowledge-transfer sessions, see the full story of GE's Global Research Centers in chapter 8.)

Such testimonials are reassuring to those guiding (or paying for) knowledge-transfer efforts, like the success stories collected in communities of practice. But testimonials say little about how much the effort closed the gap between the experts' and the learners' abilities, or how much the learners have progressed toward deeper smarts. Such assessments require disciplined, systematic attention.

## Learning Log

As recommended in chapter 6, learners working in an OPPTY-structured mentoring situation should keep a record of what they have observed, what they have done, and the results of their actions. We presented the learning log as an important part of consolidating and internalizing the deep smarts being modeled by the expert. But the learning log also serves another purpose—to track progress in learning. If that sounds like make-work, think about scuba divers, serious runners, or scientists. They all keep logs so they can chart their progress and note what the next challenge should be. Why can't we do that in knowledge-transfer situations as well? When experts and learners review the log periodically, they can figure out what additional mini-experiences would be helpful and what gaps in the learners' experience repertoires remain. This kind of systematic review of progress is one of the best ways to assess the learner's progress.

## Gap-Closure Assessments

An even more powerful way to determine if gaps in deep smarts are being narrowed over time is to use an assessment tool designed to measure that gap closure as directly as possible. The following assessment tools may superficially resemble the competence assessments described before in this chapter. But rather than assessing progress in a particular role (a soldier, a petroleum engineer), these tools address growth in experience-based expertise, specifically the dimensions of deep smarts discussed in chapter 2. Therefore, the tools are applicable across a wide variety of roles and industries.

Before we introduce these tools, keep a couple of things in mind. First, it's important to persuade the participants that the gap-closure tools are a personally useful way to gauge progress toward deep smarts, not a job performance measure. Otherwise, the assessment arouses misplaced anxiety. Second, your organization doesn't have to experience the US Army's life-or-death need for knowledge transfer in order to find it useful to check progress periodically. Both well-endowed and more frugal organizations can develop worthwhile gap-closure techniques. With these caveats in mind, we believe that it is important to strive for the best possible assessment of knowledge-gap closure and that systematically utilizing these measures will provide more convincing evidence of transfer success than troves of anecdotes and testimonials. We have designed the tool in two parts so as to enable its user to select the deep smarts that are relevant in a given situation before applying the assessment (tables 7-3 and 7-4).

Part 1 of the deep-smarts gap-assessment tool (table 7-3) is designed to determine which of the expert's generic deep-smarts dimensions are relevant for these particular learners. People in both roles are asked to rank-order the dimensions according to importance. Dimensions that are not applicable may be ignored. This task should be easy if the expert and learner have gone through the OPPTY exercise, since they will have set action plan goals based on an agreement about which know-how needs to be transferred. Part 1 of the assessment thus can be done quickly and only once, unless the goals for the transfer change.

However, it is not necessary that the expert and learner go through OPPTY to determine progress. If they have not, they can still rank-order the deep-smarts dimensions separately and then compare their rankings and negotiate which dimensions are most critical for transferring. We have discovered that there will almost always be a few dimensions that are high priority, and some that are largely irrelevant. In one setting, an expert's development and utilization of technology might be critical, while in another, perhaps

TABLE 7-3

## Deep-smarts gap-assessment tool, part 1 (as completed by Steve and Jack)

*Directions:* Rank-order each of the nine dimensions of deep smarts, according to how important they are for the learner to absorb from the expert (on a numerical rating scale, where 1 = most important and 10 = least important). Omit those that are not applicable (N/A).

| | Brief description of dimension | Rank order by learner | Rank order by expert | Final agreement |
|---|---|---|---|---|
| **COGNITIVE DIMENSIONS OF DEEP SMARTS** | | | | |
| 1. Critical skills<br>• Technical<br>• Managerial | Process and analytical skills | N/A | N/A | N/A |
| 2. System perspective<br>• Technical<br>• Organizational | Comprehension of the overall system that the work covers—not just parts of it | 6 | 7 | 7 |
| 3. Contextual awareness | Knowledge about different technology or customer situations; ability to separate signal from noise and to make fine distinctions | 1 | 1 | 1 |
| 4. Pattern recognition | Recognition of patterns—especially ones frequently encountered | 5 | 6 | 5 |
| **BEHAVIORAL DIMENSIONS** | | | | |
| 5. Networking | Extent and depth of professional network | 2 | 4 | 4 |
| 6. Interpersonal skills | Ability to collaborate, negotiate, motivate, and lead | 3 | 2 | 2 |
| 7. Communication | Ability to present material in the form required by the position | 4 | 3 | 3 |
| 8. Rapid, wise decision making | Ability to make decisions quickly but with attention to assumptions | 7 | 5 | 6 |
| 9. Diagnostic and cue seeking | Expert diagnostics; ability to extrapolate possible solutions from partial data; ability to actively seek cues that may indicate a familiar pattern | N/A | N/A | N/A |

*Note:* Steve is a possible successor to Jack, vice president of international sales for "IMC," a mining equipment company described in chapter 6.

his or her diagnostic ability needs to be emulated. Moreover, managers and subject-matter experts likely value different dimensions of deep smarts, and you don't want to shoehorn both into the same moccasin.

And there may well be dimensions for which the learner has deeper skills than the expert—especially if we are dealing with a transfer between an expert and a near expert. We have seen, for example, instances in which the intended learner was less experienced in one technical realm than the expert, but more experienced in another. In such a case, the expert's technical domain would be marked as "not applicable" in the tool, since the goal of the exercise is to transfer the deep smarts of the expert.

Let us look at how Steve (our OPPTY exemplar of a learner in a mining equipment company, discussed in chapter 6) might fill out part 1 with the help of his expert Jack and perhaps also their mutual boss or another colleague (table 7-3). Working from Steve's action plan, they agreed that seven of the nine deep-smarts dimensions were relevant. The exercise of rank ordering occasioned a lot of discussion that helped everyone agree on exactly how those dimensions applied to Steve's situation. Choosing the most and least important dimensions was relatively easy. They debated more over selection of the next top three.

Part 2 of the deep-smarts gap-assessment tool is designed to rate the learner's smarts *relative to those of the expert* on the relevant dimensions (table 7-4). That is, we calibrate the progress of the learner in terms of gaining the expert's most critical deep smarts identified in part 1 of the tool. There is no absolute standard against which the progress of knowledge transfer can be measured. We can only measure the perceived narrowing of the gap between the learner and the expert. The next task for Steve and Jack, therefore, would be to rate Steve on the individual items measuring each of the relevant dimensions. Table 7-4 presents some illustrative examples of the items associated with the top four dimensions selected by Steve and Jack in part 1 of the assessment tool. (In the full tool,

TABLE 7-4

## Deep-smarts gap-assessment tool, part 2 (partial example)

*Directions:* Compare the learner's knowledge to the expert's. Rate how comparable it is on a numerical scale from 1 to 9, where 1 = not at all comparable, 5 = moderately comparable, and 9 = completely comparable.

*Date:*

| Deep-smarts dimension | Sample item | Self-rating by learner | Rating learner by expert | Rating learner by other |
|---|---|---|---|---|
| 3. Contextual awareness (knowledge about different technology or customer contexts; ability to separate signal from noise and to make fine distinctions) | Awareness of, and sensitivity to, differences and variations from one technical/market situation to the next | | | |
| 5. Networking (extent and depth of professional network) | Extensiveness of professional network outside the organization | | | |
| 6. Interpersonal skills (ability to motivate, collaborate, negotiate, and lead ) | Ability to negotiate dispassionately and fairly | | | |
| 7. Communication (ability to present material in the form required by the position) | Ability to clearly communicate with others through oral skills | | | |

each of those dimensions is assessed with multiple items; table 7-4 presents only a few assessment items.) Steve, Jack, and perhaps another emphasized these four in recognition that Steve was technically proficient, but needed to build relationships with key dealers and understand their position in setting prices. He needed to become more fluent in presenting the competitive advantages of their products, and he would have to figure out how to negotiate pricing. All of these require the ability to communicate clearly and concisely. (If Jack and Steve worked in product design or maintenance rather than sales, the dimensions selected would probably be quite different.)

For part 2 of the gap-assessment tool to be meaningful, both the expert and the learner should fill it out immediately after completing part 1 and should fill out part 2 again at some designated interval (perhaps every six months) thereafter. If Steve and Jack fill out both parts of the tool at regular intervals, they will be able to chart Steve's progress toward the goals they have set out for him. The measures also help pinpoint where the planned mini-experiences using the OPPTY tool have failed to target some important aspects of the expert's know-how, and therefore which planned activities need adjusting. If a third person also fills out the form—for example, the designated knowledge coach, a supervisor, an internal client, or any other observer who is close enough to the work to be a good judge of progress—the assessment will be more valuable.

To return to our example, at the beginning of their mentoring relationship, Steve might rate himself 5 (moderately comparable to Jack) on "Extensiveness of professional network outside the organization," while Jack considers Steve a 3. After discussing the realities of developing a network, they might agree that Steve is indeed at the 3 level. Six months later, after actively working to further develop his professional network, Steve might now consider himself a 4, while Jack rated him a 6. The gap is being narrowed, but Steve still has a lot of network building to do to reach level 9 (completely comparable to Jack).

Once the expert and learner have had a chance to compare their responses, a third party should retain the forms each time, but not disclose them to either the expert or the learner the next time they fill out the form. (If the expert and learner are able to see how they rated the gap the last time it was measured, they are likely to be heavily influenced to make sure they have noted progress.) We suggest that the person keeping the reports *not* be in HR, so that there is less confusion between advancement toward knowledge-transfer goals and general performance reviews. Of course, the real value in such assessments lies not in simply recording numbers, but in reminding expert and learner of their goals and having discussions around what they are and could be doing to close the gap faster. By gathering this kind of data over time and across multiple learners, the organization has a systematic feedback loop that will help ascertain what smarts are being transferred and (if the learning logs are also kept) what mini-experiences in general are most effective in gap closure.

In this chapter, we have given an overview of the types of assessments professionals in the knowledge-transfer field use. All three of us have decades of experience in teaching, and we have yet to see a perfect assessment of cognitive changes because of learning. Progress is actually easier to assess in physical skills such as playing tennis, where the ball either goes where and how it is supposed to—or it doesn't. Successful knowledge transfer will be visible in behavioral changes, to be sure, but they will be less obvious. And success will look different when viewed through the eyes of the expert, the learner, and other observers. Nevertheless, a process left unexamined can easily stray from its original objectives. We believe in serious attempts to determine progress—not only to justify expenditure but also to maintain momentum.

## Questions for Managers

1. What kind of evidence of successful transfer of deep smarts from experts to less experienced employees does your upper management look for?

2. Does your organization currently assess the success of knowledge transfer? If so, how could any of the methods described in this chapter be used to augment what you already do?

3. How could learners and experts be providing systematic feedback to stakeholders on the knowledge exchanges they are involved in? How could any of the assessment methods

described in this chapter be adapted—and adopted—in your organization?

4. What could you do to collect testimonials from participants in knowledge exchanges? How could you collect evaluations of workshops and training sessions?

5. How could you encourage learners to use OPPTY-like learning logs for real-time self-assessments of learning?

6. How could you collect data about the results of knowledge exchanges through your electronic networks?

## Questions for Knowledge Recipients

1. How can you best determine whether you have deepened your expertise at work? What are some specific goals against which you can measure progress?

2. How would you use a gap-closure tool patterned after the one included in this chapter or a learning log to track the narrowing of the knowledge gap between you and experts whom you wish to emulate?

# 8

# The GE Global Research Centers Story

To illustrate some of the processes mentioned in the book, let us take a detailed look at one organization's knowledge-transfer program from its inception to ongoing implementation. General Electric's Global Research Centers (GEGRC) program does not contain all of the techniques described in the book, as the organization had the luxury of some time before critical knowledge would be permanently lost. The managers thus focused their resources on learning how to do smart questioning (with question kits) and on OPPTY.

## Background of the
## Knowledge-Transfer Project

For more than a hundred years, GEGRC has served as a resource for all of GE's businesses. The research conducted there has been responsible for innovations in a highly diverse set of technologies, from medical imaging and energy generation to jet engines and lighting. GEGRC scientists, in aggregate, have been awarded thousands of patents and are the go-to experts not only within GE, but also across industries where their research is relevant. When Boeing encountered difficulties with the batteries in its Dreamliner 787 aircraft, it sought expert solutions from, among others, GEGRC. Perhaps even more impressive, in 1988, when cold fusion was thought to be a possible source of energy, the GE board of directors asked a team of "extreme experts" to evaluate the findings of researchers Martin Fleischmann and Stanley Pons. In the end, the team found errors in the research and concluded that cold fusion was not feasible. These findings resounded across the energy industry, profoundly influencing investment decisions besides those at GE. For example, the price of the metal palladium used in the Fleischmann and Pons apparatus skyrocketed after the release of their initial findings. But when cold fusion was decisively debunked, the price dropped back to earlier levels. Therefore, retaining as much as possible of such preeminent, wide-ranging expertise was critical to GEGRC's continued success.

Prior to 2008, GEGRC followed a process that actually discouraged experts from sharing their business-critical knowledge. A scientist or an engineer would retire from the organization, wait the mandatory six months, and then field a call from a former manager with an offer to reengage. The corresponding consulting fees, combined with their pension, generated an income not too different from the person's preretirement salary, with far fewer hours worked. Retirees were simply another, albeit expensive, form of contracted labor. And the arrangement seemed like a win-win. The retiree satisfied financial and personal goals while the organization reinserted someone with unrivaled knowledge and expertise into a project and took its time sourcing replacement talent. This practice was, and remains, widespread in industry. In fact, 42 percent of the organizations in our survey reported this kind of revolving door. At Stanley Consultants engineering firm, for example, a spokeswoman explains: "They say you have the retirement party one day and you come back to work the next."[1]

So what was wrong with this picture? For one thing, at GEGRC, internal analysis predicted a potential tsunami of retirements hitting the two top technical levels between 2008 and 2013. This meant that an already costly practice could get prohibitively expensive. Worse, the rehiring agreements were structured only to provide project continuity, not to retain or transfer knowledge. After all, why would soon-to-be or recent retirees want to impart their smarts? Most of the experts wanted to be in demand (and to be paid) and to be missed when they eventually quit for good.

Ironically, the financial downturn of 2008 gave GEGRC an opportunity to change. In an effort to reduce costs, the organization forbade the rehiring of retirees in 2009. An outcry ensued, of course, but management and HR began to face the painful fact that they had been aiding and abetting a vicious cycle of capability dependency and knowledge loss.

For a while, would-be retirees simply stayed on longer than they had planned. And it was that lull in departures that allowed the organization to redesign some of its incentives, practices, and culture.[2]

In 2010, Steven Labate was manager of organization, staffing, and compensation within GEGRC's human resource organization. His manager, besieged by complaints about new restrictions on hiring back retirees to reduce costs, asked Labate to devise a solution. How could the organization continue to utilize the deep smarts of its experts, yet pass them on to their successors? The simplest solution would be to revert to the old rehiring policies. However, both managers were reluctant to take that route, because they knew it would be a temporary fix. The rehired experts would eventually leave, taking their experience and knowledge with them. No one wanted to lose that huge reservoir of deep smarts. A more inclusive and creative solution was called for.

By 2011, Labate had developed a program to retain and transfer deep smarts, some objectives of which were as follows:

- Retain high-performing, experienced workers longer through the implementation of flexible work arrangements.

- Transfer expert's technical skills to other employees prior to the expert's retirement.

- Develop practices to better utilize retirees.

Labate's first move was to figure out how severe the problem was. Diving into employment data, he found that much of the US-based principal and chief engineer or scientist population at GEGRC was indeed nearing retirement age. The issue was not confined to GE. From conversations with HR colleagues across the United States, he knew that many companies—especially those that were long established and had highly technical staff—were facing a huge wave of retirements. But how to identify just where the greatest loss of expertise was likely? The biggest challenges were to make sure the program was aimed at where it could do the most good and to address the need to transfer critical knowledge, without seeming arbitrary.

## Identifying Knowledge at Risk of Loss

Knowing that engineers and scientists at GEGRC would feel more comfortable using a familiar set of metrics, Labate asked each US laboratory manager to quantify various types of risk related to loss of knowledge according to a metric called quality function deployment (QFD). The QFD system usually applied to engineering design, but was also adaptable to this situation. (For an example of a similar quantitative approach, refer back to the Baker Hughes example in chapter 3.) The GEGRC lab managers considered each employee in their organization in a senior, principal, or chief role. As table 8-1 shows, the numbers 1, 3, and 9 represented different levels of risk (low, moderate, or high) along various dimensions: demand for the expertise, supply of it (i.e., current availability within GEGRC), the criticality of the expertise to the business, risk from lack of succession planning, availability of skills from external sources, and risk

TABLE 8-1

## Assessing and addressing vulnerability to knowledge loss at GE's Global Research Centers (GEGRC), step 1

*Quantify capability risk through a quality function deployment (QFD) approach.*

| | Demand Immediacy | Supply GEGRC current capability | Employee criticality based on skill mastery | Succession planning | External skill set availability | Attrition risk before [date] |
|---|---|---|---|---|---|---|
| **Scale** | 9 Strong<br>3 Moderate<br>1 Weak | 9 Minimal or single point<br>3 Sufficient depth<br>1 Recognized depth | 9 High<br>3 Moderate<br>1 Low | 9 No formal plan in place<br>3 Plan in place with some execution<br>1 Plan with strong execution; or no plan needed | 9 Difficult; lengthy search likely<br>3 Moderate difficulty<br>1 Low level of difficulty | 9 High<br>3 Moderate<br>1 Low |
| **Rating** | 9 | 3 | 9 | 9 | 3 | 3 |
| **Total** | 36 | | | | | |

*Note*: Rating using an example of an employee, "John Smith," from electrochemistry.

of an individual's leaving within the next four years. The ratings on these dimensions aggregated to a risk score for each employee. Total scores above 30 were considered high. In the example in table 8-1, the cumulative score of 36 for "John Smith," the example we used, indicated very high risk.

Next, Labate determined what skills, in general terms, individuals with high scores possessed and what was being done to pass those skills along (see, e.g., table 8-2). Forty-six percent of the employees reviewed had scores over 30. In many cases, Labate found, the researchers were already working together in an informal form of the OPPTY process. That is, experts were working closely in a project with a colleague whose research interests and abilities coincided well enough that there was a natural exchange of knowledge. But for other researchers, there was no obvious successor; their deep smarts would be lost to GEGRC when the researcher retired.

TABLE 8-2

**Assessing and addressing vulnerability to knowledge loss at GE's Global Research Centers (GEGRC), step 2**

*Prioritize vulnerabilities by conducting a capability analysis for individuals at high risk (risk score above 30; see table 8-1) for knowledge loss.*

| Score | Employee | Capability area | Key skill(s) | Strategy to address vulnerability |
|---|---|---|---|---|
| 36 | Smith, John | Membrane and separation technology | Electrochemistry | Staff project X such that junior scientist is paired with John Smith |

# Selecting a Strategy

In looking around at other organizations facing similar retirement bulges, Labate found that many other companies were confronting the same issue. Some organizations were more proactive than others, but very few seemed to have a strategy that was both proactive and integrated with its overall human resource strategy. Labate decided to raise awareness of the issue at GEGRC's January 2012 Global Leadership Meeting, an annual gathering of the top 200 GEGRC managers and technical leaders from around the globe. What Labate hoped to accomplish with this meeting was to educate all on the gravity of the problem and set the stage for new initiatives designed to mitigate knowledge-loss risk due to retirements. Elevating this topic into the meeting agenda suggested the urgency of the problem. He therefore invited one of us (Dorothy) to address the topic at the meeting.

The message was well received, with managers quick to grasp the costs of losing knowledge. Although methods for capturing and transferring that knowledge were not yet clear, Labate was mindful that the deeply smart scientists and engineers at GEGRC not only were preeminent in their technical fields, but also had a wealth of know-how, professional networks, and skills based on many years of experience. Their decisions were driven not only by reference to scientific first principles but by the needs and priorities of their primary clients inside GE, such as GE Aviation and GE Energy, and those of the government agencies that funded the research. Many scientists were exceptional communicators and inspiring team leaders who motivated their research teams to excel. Therefore not only was technical wizardry at risk when the scientists retired, but so also were their deep smarts in designing, funding, and conducting the research.

Conceptually, Labate found the prior research on deep smarts convincing, but what he needed were practical next steps. He was confident that GEGRC had a lot of internal consulting and educational skills that could be developed further and directed at the program. Therefore he wanted to embed an ongoing knowledge-sharing capability within GEGRC. Even after the initial baby-boomer bulge of retirements was addressed, there were many older, highly experienced personnel at the senior engineer level (below principal and chief). The challenge of preserving GEGRC's deep smarts was not going to disappear.

He therefore moved toward the strategy suggested in chapter 4: "hiring a fisherman" to train internal personnel how to fish. GEGRC hired the Leonard-Barton Group to pilot a knowledge-transfer workshop and train GEGRC personnel to take over after the process that was tailored to GEGRC's needs had been standardized. Labate enlisted the help of change initiatives leader, Tim O'Hara, who had many years of experience in organizational design and leadership curriculum development. Once the process was proven, O'Hara would bring it in house. He would take over directing additional workshops and monitoring the progress of the project.

The major immediate objectives for the workshop were to enhance the effectiveness and efficiency of those mentoring processes already in place and to enhance the design of new knowledge-sharing relationships by providing a basic understanding of the nature of knowledge and of best practices in transferring knowledge. The long-term objectives were to help GEGRC develop the desired internal capability to design knowledge-transfer programs and to help avoid the costs of knowledge loss.

Labate soon discovered that the workshop involved a lot of preliminary work.

## Triads: Expert, Learner, and Coach

The workshop designed for GEGRC called for the participants to work in triads consisting of an expert, a learner, and a process coach. Each of these individuals had to be identified and persuaded to participate. Of immediate concern was what to call the second role. While new hires might not mind being thought of as mentees or learners, many of the logical successors in this case had fifteen years or more under their belts and were experts or mentors in their own rights— just not quite as experienced as the experts whose knowledge was at risk. Labate decided to call this group *near experts*, and the term stuck. But if the near expert wasn't interested in learning more about the expert's field—game over! So the near expert's willingness to learn had to be assessed and encouraged. Matching the right expert with the right successors was essential, because both parties had to be motivated to spend time on the knowledge exchange.

Finding process coaches, whose role would be to help the expert and near expert with any problems that might arise during the workshop, and more importantly, after it, was even more challenging. The coach role was created to address a wide range of implementation issues, from scheduling knowledge-transfer sessions to interpersonal issues, obtaining resources, or monitoring the fulfillment of the expert and near expert agreements with each other.

Not all knowledge-transfer situations require process coaches; the role can also be assumed by consultants if necessary. However, such coaches were deemed important at GEGRC for a number of reasons—primarily to share the responsibility for forward momentum in the knowledge-transfer program. The list of recommended characteristics for the knowledge-sharing coach at GEGRC required an unusual blend of skills:

- Credibility in the organization

- Interest in knowledge transfer, and willingness to learn about cognitive theory, transfer techniques, and pitfalls

- Experience with, and interest in, some kind of coaching or teaching

- Technical expertise—but not in the area of the expert in the triad, if possible (to avoid the coach's taking on the role of expert)

- Interpersonal communication skills

- Ability to subordinate their own egos, that is, having no need to impress

In a highly technical organization such as GEGRC, credibility meant a high level of education, technical expertise, and a good research track record. Such individuals, of course, were much in demand; there were many calls on their time. However, if process coaches lacked the credibility prized by the organization, they could be relegated to a clerical scheduling function. In contrast, credible, successful individuals who believed in the process were powerful advocates and kept the knowledge-transfer interactions from being overwhelmed by urgent daily work. Labate therefore went to work identifying and recruiting a set of high-level coaches. The first group of coaches consisted of technical leaders; one coach was even a second-level manager responsible for a global technology organization. Most were experienced mentors, and some had taught courses inside and out of GEGRC. The selected individuals committed not only to a few hours of preparation and a full day of workshop, but also to an indeterminate quantity of follow-up time. As we will see later, several coaches became caught up in the program and dedicated to its success.

# Preliminary Work

Once everyone was selected, the HR team sent out memos about the upcoming workshop. Memos turned out to be inadequate to explain the whole process—particularly the request that every expert participate in an hour-long interview with Transition-Path to produce a BroadScope, a visual map of their roles, responsibilities, and regular tasks (see chapter 4). Some participants were initially reluctant to agree to the requisite hour, but most found the BroadScope interview an interesting exercise and rather pleasing to the ego, since it showed how much work they did!

The experts shared their visual maps of how they spent their time with their corresponding near expert before and during the workshop. In later workshops, Tim O'Hara worked with Transition-Path to narrow the focus and further deepen the coverage of the BroadScope to emphasize the technical expertise that GEGRC wished to preserve. O'Hara's involvement helped the expert and the interviewer to better connect and the Transition-Path interviewer to better understand the scope of technology and duties carried out by the expert. Participants were also asked to read a very short "case" written about knowledge-sharing issues at an anonymous (but suspiciously familiar-sounding) research facility and to read an article in *Harvard Business Review* on deep smarts. Rather than waiting until the day of the workshop to explain its objectives, O'Hara met with all workshop participants before the actual workshop to provide them with an overview of the upcoming workshop and to answer their questions.

# The Workshop

The Leonard-Barton Group team conducted two one-day workshops, four months apart. The workshop was positioned and described to the participants as the first step in a journey.

The objectives were to introduce a shared vocabulary, to create some common understanding of how knowledge transfer differs from other kinds of educational exchange, to set expectations about the roles for members of the triads, and to provide tools for ongoing work. The sessions were divided among conceptual presentations, explanation of tools, and practice using the tools, thus alternating between less interactive sessions and hands-on exercises. Here is an abbreviated version of the agenda:

*Introduction:* Agenda and the objectives for the day

*Session 1:* Introduction to roles (expert, near expert, and knowledge-sharing coach) and to observation templates for knowledge-sharing coaches

*Session 2:* Case discussion

*Session 3:* Presentation of deep smarts and knowledge-sharing fundamentals

*Session 4:* Agreement (contract); OPPTY action plan

*Session 5:* Introduction to knowledge elicitation and practice using tools in two of the question kits

*Session 6:* Monitoring progress, and debrief and review of all tools, including learning log and gap-closure assessments

*Session 7:* Knowledge-sharing coaches meet in a separate training session

As might be expected when a novel, likely time-consuming program is introduced, GEGRC participants entered with a healthy dose of skepticism. Being researchers themselves, they were somewhat mollified by the explanations of the research-based psychological and cognitive bases for the workshop. Those who were already skilled mentors or the recipients of good mentoring were the most receptive, recognizing the value of the best practices suggested.

For example, when the value of OPPTY was challenged in one workshop, a coach spoke up: "That's exactly what my mentor did, and I wouldn't be here today if he had not exposed me to so many valuable experiences. For example, he took me with him on customer site visits and introduced me to some of his best contacts. This *works!*"

The workshop took a whole day (8:30 a.m. to 4:30 p.m.) with sessions of varying lengths. A total of seventeen tools were reviewed and practiced, including a relationships (networking) tool, a deep-smarts identification tool, and an OPPTY action plan.

## The Contract

Preparation for a knowledge-transfer process includes ensuring that there is agreement on the knowledge to be transferred, the purpose of the transfer, and the resources to be used. Part of workshop session 4 was devoted to reviewing a working plan agreement (a so-called contract) between expert and near expert, with the stated intent of getting both parties' bosses to sign off on the resources allocated—particularly time (table 8-3).

Coaches were asked to follow up to make sure that the contract was reviewed with the managers of both experts and near experts. For the most part, this turned out to be unnecessary. Once the managers had signed off on the idea that the expert would be working with a near expert, they left it largely up to the expert to allocate the time. Because most of the pairs were able to work together on projects, that is, on "real work," no extra time needed to be allocated. When that kind of pairing was not possible and the near expert was expected to complete his or her own work and still find time to elicit knowledge from the expert, the transfer process was much slower. But even in such cases, the pairs found time to meet every couple of weeks to discuss problems and to allow the near expert some time to elicit knowledge.

TABLE 8-3

## Example of an agreement (a contract) between expert and near expert

| Topic and description | Agreement between expert and near expert |
|---|---|
| ULTIMATE GOAL FOR NEAR EXPERT | BECOME THE "GO-TO" PERSON ON RECIPROCATING ENGINE TECHNOLOGY |
| Criteria for ultimate goal:<br>• Identifies exact domains of knowledge to be targeted<br>• Describes an end state—what success looks like<br>• Is realistic within the given time frame<br>• Recognizes that there is real business value in having the near expert reach this goal<br>• Will be accepted as reasonable by affected parties | The near expert will:<br>• Learn new advances in technology<br>• Understand the field and develop a professional network<br>• Become established as expert and be seen as such by others in the organization |
| TIME FRAME FOR ACHIEVING ULTIMATE GOAL: TARGET END DATE | GOAL TO BE ACHIEVED IN 24–30 MONTHS |
| • Sets target end date<br>• Identifies possible additional time constraints<br>• Estimates hours per week available for the expert, near expert, and coach | • Constraints; current and future projects<br>• Buy-in from technology leaders needed<br>• Expert and near expert meet three hours per week<br>• Near expert and coach meet for an hour every two weeks; triad meets for an hour once a month |
| INTERACTION OPTIONS (NOT MUTUALLY EXCLUSIVE) | APPLY OPPTY OPTIONS, QUESTION KITS, GAP-CLOSURE TOOLS |
| • Work together (on projects or problem solving), using OPPTY<br>• Intermittent interaction possibilities:<br>  • During specific office hours<br>  • Open-door policy (i.e., anytime)<br>  • During lunches<br>• Knowledge-elicitation sessions<br>• Other? | • Observation<br>• Practice<br>• Partner<br>• Take responsibility<br>• Knowledge-elicitation session on current project<br>• Informal lunches together once a month<br>• Fill out gap-closure tools every six months |
| SIGN-OFF BY UPPER MANAGEMENT | |

## Starting to Fish

By the end of the two workshops, GEGRC's change initiatives leader, Tim O'Hara, was ready to take over, with the help of the detailed instructor manual the consultants provided. He brought in as instructors participants from the two prior workshops. These individuals not only added credibility to the process, drawn as they were from the ranks of highly respected scientists and engineers, but also were enthusiastic missionaries and session facilitators. O'Hara also persuaded the sponsoring technology manager of each group to address the workshop participants first thing in the morning, reinforcing the importance of the program.

## Indicators of Success

The GEGRC workshops are an ongoing responsibility for O'Hara, who has proven that they are replicable. He receives continued reinforcement from alumni of the process. While, of course, there is variation in the speed with which the near experts have been able to demonstrate that they are internalizing the knowledge passed along to them, there is significant progress in almost all the triads. As one expert noted, "the near expert is becoming the go-to guy; he's making great progress." Asked how he knew there was such progress, he said, "I base my assessment on his answers to my questions." A near expert similarly reported that "the business is recognizing me as an up-and-coming expert." There is good evidence that the pairs are using workshop suggestions about how to learn most effectively. For example, a near expert reported engaging in the discovery method of learning. In addressing an unknown topic, she now first tells the expert what she would do and *then* asks what he would do. "This has been very valuable," she said. Most teams follow the OPPTY process, creating deliberate opportunities for guided experience that wouldn't otherwise occur, such as attending conferences and being introduced to the expert's networks, or taking over from the expert parts of in-house instruction in technological specialties. Other participants are finding naturally occurring opportunities within the project structure for the kinds of observation, practice, and joint problem solving recommended.

## Some Lessons Learned at GEGRC

As O'Hara has remarked, this is not a one-shot, put-your-nickel-in-and-get-your-ride process. He knew this going in, intellectually at least—but he is frequently reminded that this program of knowledge transfer is ongoing and requires continuous nurturing and monitoring. And he keeps needing to remind the participants of this point. The OPPTY process in particular requires more than a couple months of joint work. Ideally, the experts and near experts work together on a project, and setting up those projects takes time.

Matching experts and one or more near experts can be tricky. One primary consideration is the gap mentioned in chapter 3. The wider the gap between the expert and the near expert, the more difficult the knowledge transfer. Near experts who lack basic understanding may have to bone up a bit before they have the receptors for the expert's deep smarts. On the other hand, near experts sometimes feel that they know just as much as, or more than, the expert in some domains, so the coach has to help the duo focus on a gap that the near expert *wants* to close. The relationship between the duo must be carefully created and nurtured if no prior one exists. A good interpersonal relationship and mutual trust are essential to knowledge sharing. And all the duos need to be open to *two-way flows* of knowledge.

GEGRC discovered that focusing on just one working group at a time for each workshop provided important benefits. First, having everyone from the same basic disciplines aids the administration of the BroadScope interview and helps workshop instructors understand the specialized team vocabularies. Second, with a single working group, there is just one leader from whom to seek the approval and the time allocation for both preliminary work and the workshop. Moreover, this leader is also involved, of course, in identifying the members of the triad and especially in helping to match experts and near experts.

Leadership in the organization has to reinforce the importance of the effort both with words and with actions. For example, one GEGRC leader, hearing that there was no obvious opportunity for joint work by an expert with the selected near expert, deliberately created a project for them to work on together. The leader's involvement is also critical for an accounting of progress from the expert and near expert.

If organizations follow the model that the Leonard-Barton Group set up for GEGRC, which includes the role of knowledge coach, those process coaches need to be selected very carefully. As mentioned earlier, problems can arise when a coach has the same expertise as the expert. While, of course, the learner benefits from the wisdom of two individuals, the coach role may get slighted and the expert may feel his or her role has been usurped. Therefore, the Leonard-Barton Group suggests that the coach be highly respected in the organization and highly capable in the knowledge valued in the organization (which may mean being technically very proficient). However, it works best for the coach to have expertise in a different work area from that of the designated expert. GEGRC's coaches met those criteria. Also, it is much easier for coaches to play their role if they are colocated with the expert and learner—or at least with one of them, preferably the learner. One of the coaches' important tasks is to ensure that the knowledge targeted for exchange matches organizational needs.

## Other Generic Lessons Learned

GEGRC undertook a particular approach, and some of the lessons derived are specific to that approach. But a few, more general lessons can be derived from both GEGRC's experience and that of others using different transfer techniques.

The first critical step in any transfer initiative is to determine what part of a person's know-how is to be targeted for transfer. As noted before, not all of an expert's knowledge is worth capturing. Some knowledge may be outdated; some may not be rare or limited to a small set of experts but is readily available in the industry. The selection process is too important to be left to just the expert and successors. Neither type of individual is likely to have the broad overview to make that determination. Experts understandably may have passion for some of their work that is not essential to future organizational needs or may not realize that some of their skills are actually available elsewhere in the organization. Involving other leaders and senior knowledge coaches helps ensure that the knowledge selected is indeed critical. Moreover, the more specific the description of the skills to be transferred, the better. "Ability to oversee the manufacture of a new-design nuclear reactor tube" is better than "understand metal machining processes."

Some experts' knowledge is so broad and deep that two or more successors may be needed to fill just one pair of high heels. After many years on the job, executives often have more responsibilities than any one person should be expected to handle—and certainly more expertise than a less experienced soul can absorb. One executive we know in a highly regulated industry wears two hats—one hat concentrated in regulation and the other in legal. Either one of these responsibilities alone is a full-time job. If and when she leaves, it is unlikely that one person will take on both areas. And in technical organizations, perhaps surprisingly, successors are often at least as interested in learning their more experienced colleagues' soft skills, such as leading and motivating teams, as they are in the technical aspects of the job that they can learn elsewhere. In such cases, the transfer effort can focus on just a part of the incumbent's deep smarts—or on identifying several successors for different aspects of the expert's role.

But not all of the expert's smarts may be deep. Highly skilled people may be handling affairs that could be delegated to less experienced and less skilled individuals—permanently. One of the strongest drivers of outsourcing has been the tantalizing possibility of shifting routine knowledge work to outside offices. Some organizations are finding that even knowledge work more essential to their primary mission can also be reallocated so as to free up highly specialized subject-matter experts to address only the most critical work. For example, highly paid lawyers pass along work that doesn't require their expertise to paralegals or less specialized lawyers in less expensive locations; clinical and administrative responsibilities of specialist physicians could be shifted to nurses, paramedics, and assistant practitioners.[3]

Finally, the benefits of any initiative requiring effort and budget will clearly be greatest wherever the problem to be addressed is most acute. As with any program of change, people have first to be aware of the problem before they can be expected to address it, let alone commit resources to solving it. Start where the pain is felt— and seek some early wins. One reason that we suggest some ways to quickly demonstrate knowledge capture (as, for example, through the critical-incident sessions) is to create the requisite visibility of both problem and possible solutions. In the next chapter, we address some starting points for your transfer initiative and discuss the obstacles that you may need to clear away to succeed.

# 9

# Socializing the Organization

The HR executive in a large retailer came back from her meeting with upper management feeling victorious. She had presented arguments in support of launching a knowledge-transfer initiative, and the attendees were receptive to her explanation of the costs of losing deep smarts. "Most of the training we do is 'nice to have,'" she told us. "This knowledge transfer is '*need* to have' training. Makes it easier to justify the expense. But"—she paused in thought—"I still have a lot of work to do to get everyone on board." She explained that dictates from on high could be viewed skeptically as one more temporary enthusiasm, one more program that diverted attention from daily operations. Now she had to get the support of the experts, the learners, potential facilitators—and most important, the businesses that would have to find funds in their budgets. So there were some challenges ahead to selling the program throughout the organization.

By this time in the book, we hope that you have identified some knowledge-sharing approaches, some tools and techniques that you would like to try in your own team or organization. But you can't wave a wand and make it happen. There are a lot of people who have to buy in to this effort. People designing knowledge-transfer initiatives often speak of them as "change management," and the more obstacles to knowledge sharing that your organization has built into its DNA, the more that characterization holds true. So in this final chapter, we look at what people in your role tell us are some of the major obstacles to be overcome to manage that change—and we suggest some solutions.

## Does the Organizational Culture Support Knowledge Sharing?

Your starting point for a knowledge-transfer initiative will depend heavily on the organizational culture. Some cultures promote open exchanges of knowledge, while others can be much more resistant.

"Of course. It's part of our culture." The individual's response to a request to share knowledge can be warmly welcomed when employees are wedded to a corporate mission or when teaching and learning are the "way things are done here." In such cultures, we find people who expect and want to give back, to leave a legacy.

Consider, for example a situation in which you might reasonably expect a negative response to a request to teach successors the secrets of a person's expertise. A multinational medical device firm made the strategic decision to consolidate the European research, development, support, and customer service operations for one of its device platforms to its US location. The experts in each of these European operations were asked to work with consulting firm K.L. Hagen and Associates to transfer their expertise to the US group, which would result ultimately in the relocating or letting go of those experts. A natural reaction of these people could have ranged from bemusement at the request to open resistance. A few did have such responses. However, a majority were willing to transfer their knowledge because they believed in the mission of their organization.

They were proud of their innovations and cared deeply about both their doctor clients and the patients who received their devices. Because these experts wanted to pass along a legacy, they wanted the transfer to succeed.

Couple this kind of pride in work with an expectation that success depends on continuous improvement, and team pay depends upon team output, and you have the knowledge-sharing culture found at Nucor Steel. Founder Ken Iverson built a company where profitability depends on everyone's being a learner and a teacher. Growth through acquisition therefore required transferring not only operational know-how but the culture as well (see the sidebar "Nucor Steel's Tuscaloosa Turnaround").

# Nucor Steel's Tuscaloosa Turnaround

When Nucor Steel acquired a coiled-plate mill in Tuscaloosa, Alabama, in July 2004, the acquisition faced a number of challenges. The acquired mill's safety record was very poor; turnover was high, and production was under 700,000 tons per year. The plant had not turned a profit in over eight years.

By 2013, the plant was turning out more than one million tons, safety was one of the best in Nucor, and the plant had been consistently profitable since 2004 (except for 2009, during the Great Recession). Perhaps most impressive was that the plant had become a source of talent for the rest of the company.

What explained that dramatic about-face? The transfer of Nucor culture, with six distinct characteristics:

- Careful choice of people
- Clear direction and expected outcomes

Established norms of collaboration, with carefully defined values

- Tools for success, with training in everything from environmental safety to leadership skills

- Responsibility pushed down to the lowest levels of the organization

- Personal accountability to teammates and the company

The personnel at Tuscaloosa had a great deal to learn in a short period of time. They had to learn new safety systems and how to do root-cause analysis. One of the biggest challenges, as with all Nucor acquisitions, was to demonstrate to employees that Nucor's pay-for-performance approach and emphasis on teamwork in production would not hurt their wallets. Rather than just immediately switch them to Nucor's payment system, the company paid Tuscaloosa employees as they always had been—but they were also shown in dollars and cents how much more, on average, they would have earned under the Nucor system.

Much of this new knowledge was conveyed by seasoned Nucor employees at every level of the plant, through on-the-job training. Tuscaloosa teammates also traveled to other plants, as Nucor's highly collegial culture emphasizes face-to-face learning.[a]

a. Katherine Miller, Nucor Steel communications manager, email to author (DL), October 8, 2013; Josh Wall, Nucor Steel Leadership and Organizational Development Manager, telephone interview with authors (DL, WS), June 8, 2013.

Nucor and the medical device firm have a number of cultural characteristics in common, including a sense of shared mission and strong team relationships. Numerous studies have found that a willingness to share knowledge depends on *trust*—trust based on strong interpersonal relationships, leading to the conviction that what you share will not be abused. For example, in a study of knowledge transfer between firms in a joint venture, researchers found that the transfer of tacit knowledge (and the ultimate success of the alliance) was strongly related to perceptions of trustworthiness of the partner.[1]

## Clearing the Way

So are we left with the conclusion that knowledge sharing depends entirely on the intent and wisdom of the organizational founders—for better or worse? That's sort of akin to saying your personal destiny depends on your choice of parents. But just as genes are only part of our life determinants, our initial organizational culture is only a starting point. There will almost always be obstacles to knowledge sharing, and once we recognize those obstacles, we can formulate strategies to overcome them. If your organization is one whose culture already encourages knowledge sharing, then the obstacles are easier to remove. As Teresa Amabile and Steven Kramer have written in *The Progress Principle*, when teams are intrinsically motivated, "what management really had to do . . . was to remove the barriers that could have impeded that existing motivation—barriers like distraction from irrelevant tasks."[2] Their extensive research demonstrated that many times, people's natural, intrinsically motivated desire to do their job or move a project along is stifled because of obstacles that can be addressed—and that the most important help managers can give is to clear the way. This point is reinforced in an account of a popular approach to accelerating project work (see the sidebar "Removing Obstacles at Medco").

So what barriers might impede your progress in transferring knowledge? In chapter 1, we described the survey we conducted with CTOs, CIOs, and HR executives. In that survey, we asked the respondents to identify the most important obstacles to knowledge

# Removing Obstacles at Medco

In 2007, Medco (since merged with Express Scripts), the largest online pharmacy in the world, was about to undertake a major initiative designed to cut costs while providing a more positive experience for customers. Medco's president had publically announced a firm date for completing the extremely complex software redesign necessitated by the initiative, and that date appeared unrealistically optimistic. Jeff Sutherland was brought in to apply the Scrum methodology he had cocreated for accelerating projects. The assignment: deliver by the publicized date. Part of the Scrum methodology is identification and removal of impediments to completing projects. The Medco team identified twelve impediments to progress, ranging from lackadaisical meeting attendance by some members to various technical requirements. A senior vice president, who had worked at Toyota and embraced that company's similar ideology of removing impediments to productivity, took the list and distributed it to his team with a manager's name attached to each item. In three days, every obstacle had been removed. Weeks were shaved off the delivery time.[a]

a. Jeff Sutherland, *Scrum: The Art of Doing Twice the Work in Half the Time* (New York: Crown Business, 2014).

transfer in their organizations. Figure 9-1 displays the four most frequently mentioned.

## *There Is No Time!*

Overall, experts' lack of time to mentor was seen as the most significant obstacle to sharing knowledge by our survey respondents,

FIGURE 9-1

## Obstacles to knowledge transfer

*Percentage of survey respondents citing each obstacle as number one or number two in their organization.*

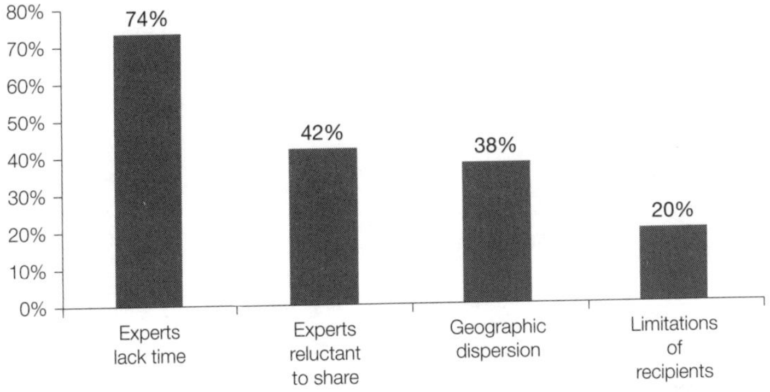

with 74 percent reporting it was either the most or the second-most important. The issues on our desks requiring immediate attention often supersede the longer-term, but critical ones. And with companies reluctant to hire after the Great Recession, many high-level executives, scientists, and engineers were working flat-out at the time of the survey—often having taken on the responsibilities of departed colleagues. Finding time to address needs such as coaching or mentoring your successor—needs that are not causing immediate work stoppage, even though they may have serious long-term consequences—is a perennial problem.

One of the reasons that we suggest some short-term knowledge acquisition techniques focused on implicit knowledge in chapter 4 is that these can be used to demonstrate some early value. If the time spent on knowledge transfer is perceived as an investment rather than just pure cost, experts and learners are more willing to spend precious time, and stakeholders to allocate resources. For example, in one organization we know, the critical-incident technique has been used in a weekly series of meetings between a retiring expert and learners, focused on some critical events during which the expert played a central role. Facilitated by a knowledge-sharing coach who is senior in the organization, these sessions take relatively little time, but have proven very valuable to all attendees. And the designated learners have become increasingly adroit at asking probing questions that reveal the expert's decision-making processes.

There are other ways to counter the lack of time. Some teams of experts and learners at GEGRC, for example, have managed to shape projects so that the learner is an immediate contributor and coworker. In other situations, experts have been able to offload some responsibilities that were essential to the organization but that no longer required their thirty years of experience. In one specific example, a senior manager who traditionally represents the organization on an industry council decided to help a junior colleague to make valuable contacts by accompanying the expert to council meetings. After a few such meetings in which the learner demonstrated considerable knowledge about recent changes in the competitive environment, the expert decided that his younger colleague added more value than he himself did.

If experts are so buried in current obligations that they simply have no time to pass their knowledge along, at least you want to be sure that the deep smarts don't totally leave the organization when those folks retire. As the GEGRC story illustrated, hiring back retirees to continue at the same job is not a good way to preserve deep smarts. But hiring back (or retaining) retirees for the express purpose of imparting their knowledge is a wise investment—and addresses the issue of time constraints by taking pressure off current employees. Usually the retirees' workload is lighter than before they retired, giving them added incentive to mentor.

At Xerox, when the retirement of a critical employee occupying a unique role, for example, a systems administrator, is announced well in advance, the impact of the departure is assessed, and a decision is made whether to retain the person's knowledge and, if so, how to do it. A number of accommodations may be made to facilitate the transfer of knowledge. The retiree's workweek may be shortened (without a corresponding cut in salary) and his or her transition period may be extended to train a replacement. The outgoing person may also agree to be available via phone for the successor for a period after retirement.

At another company whose CIO we interviewed, retiring managers and executives stay on the payroll for an additional twelve months, and their primary responsibility becomes mentoring their replacement. They may come in to the office only one day a week, but it is understood that they are always available for questions by their successor, usually dealing with unstructured (implicit) information about suppliers and customers, for example. According to the CIO, the process goes smoothly, and the exiting manager is very willing to answer a phone call requesting help, because it is now a part of the job.

## Experts Reluctant to Share

The CIOs, CTOs, and HR executives who completed our survey identified two sources of their experts' reluctance to share: the lack of incentives to teach or coach, and the view that their expertise confers power and status and therefore should be hoarded. These two sources of resistance by experts to sharing their deep smarts constitute the second-most cited obstacle, with 42 percent of the respondents rating it either the first or second-most important.

We have seen up close the resistance to share, and it's not pretty.

"Why would I want to do that?" The question was in response to our query "When you left your position as an experienced aircraft maintenance engineer, did you spend any time mentoring or teaching someone else what you knew?" The respondent, Dennis, went on to explain that he felt no obligation to help either his replacement or the organization for which he had worked for thirty-plus years. "Let me tell you," he said bitterly, "my mentor, George, taught me everything I know. He knew *everything* about aircraft maintenance. He was the guy anyone could go to with questions—and he always took time to help you. But the organization pushed him out. They never acknowledged him the way they should have. Never supported his mentoring. No recognition at all. I owe them *nothing*. Did they miss me when I retired? I sure hope so!"

Dennis is not alone in his bitter refusal to impart his expertise when he retired. Two separate (but similar) responses to a blog about GEGRC's new policy of not hiring back retirees as consultants vividly illustrate the cynicism—and anger—that the expectation of sharing knowledge can provoke in a toxic culture:

> *Any experienced expert or manager isn't going to give away his/ her experience for free, even if they practically could. Most "mentoring" is just about ego stroking and building power relationships. Ultimately in the current business world, if you want someone to impart value and effort—you are just going to have to pay them— and if they are smart that person will always hold something back to maintain some illusion of value.*
>
> *. . . Here is what "experience" teaches you—you better look after yourself and your own wallet—because a company or some manager (especially a younger manager looking to make a mark) will screw you as soon as look at you . . . someone will always try and minimize an older worker's knowledge and value.*[3]

If experts in your organization have this kind of attitude, what can you do? You probably know that there are two kinds of motivations that come into play when people are asked to share knowledge: intrinsic and extrinsic.[4] Intrinsic motivation may come from a desire to leave a legacy or from enjoyment of teaching and mentoring—or even just from the opportunity to show off a bit! Extrinsic comes in the form of recognition, pressure to perform, or monetary rewards. Even if you can't change the culture of your entire organization, you can work to stimulate more of the intrinsic and to find ways to offer extrinsic rewards.

## Stimulating Intrinsic Motivation

Intrinsic motivation can't be forced. But people sometimes want to do something—they just don't want to be told *how*. That is, they may accept an objective as legitimate, but achieve it their own way.

Kent Greenes, founder of Greenes Consulting, tells a story very revealing of human nature: Greenes was working with an oil company that had a community of practice focused on well completion—all those tasks to be done after drilling, including setting and cementing the casing that ensures the integrity and stability of the well. Most of the experienced subject-matter experts were open to sharing, but one old-timer objected. He said he did not have the time and seemed uninterested in sharing: "I'm too busy; just let me do my job." After exhausting all the usual arguments about the benefits to the company of capturing experience, Greenes gave up. Yet a couple days later, he happened to pass the elder's open door and was surprised to see four young workers sitting on the floor in the expert's office, watching him draw diagrams on his whiteboard and sharing his knowledge. For this man (and undoubtedly a lot of others in other organizations), leaving a legacy did motivate sharing—but only on his own time, in his own way.[5]

## Combining Intrinsic with Extrinsic

Ideally, as research on motivation shows, a combination of both intrinsic and extrinsic motivation is more effective than either by itself, particularly when the incentives reinforce people's internal motives.[6] Some managers have applied that understanding to stimulating knowledge flows.

At global adhesives provider H.B. Fuller, for example, the chief technology and innovation officer, Hassan Rmaile, introduced a mentoring program with ten senior chemical specialists paired with ten recent recruits. Mentors received a number of extrinsic rewards for their participation. For example, one senior specialist went to Shanghai to mentor for three weeks, taking his wife along.

And when he returned, he was given a onetime cash award. But in addition to these perks, Rmaile spoke with the experts about the value of leaving a legacy: "Thirty years from now, this person will still be talking about how much he learned from you." He finds that this appeal to intrinsic motivation is persuasive in encouraging mentoring.[7]

In our survey, 27 percent of the respondents reported that there were specific incentives for knowledge sharing or mentoring. Of those, several pointed to direct (extrinsic) incentives such as cash bonuses or the inclusion of mentoring in performance goals or learning objectives. The latter are particularly effective, because the incentive is baked into succession planning.

Kiho Sohn, principal of Sohn Consulting, described a program at a major aerospace company where experts can volunteer to share their knowledge and are matched on an internal website with those who wish to be mentored. Sounds pretty intrinsic, but to move up the technical ladder from associate to senior fellow, an employee must have mentored someone. So there are also clear, extrinsic reasons for the experts to enter into a mentoring relationship.[8]

Similarly at Schlumberger Business Consulting, engineers on its six-level technical ladder can't climb to the next rung without proving they have contributed to community knowledge. When individuals believe they are ready for the next step, they self-nominate and submit a document in support. One of the five areas covered is mentoring and community leadership, including sharing technical knowledge within their areas of concentration. Contributions can be face-to-face or electronic. So, for example, one individual wrote: "I conducted two one-week training schools in 2009 where a total of 25 engineers from the United States and Canada were introduced to the YY product. The objective was to familiarize engineers in the North American area with the science of microseismic monitoring. The students were exposed to theory and practical exercises that discussed operational procedures, measurement physics, and microseismic evaluation."[9]

## Geographic Dispersion

Thirty-eight percent of our survey respondents reported that their geographically dispersed workforce created either their number one or number two obstacle to knowledge transfer. One of the primary ways that organizations are addressing this obstacle is by connecting groups of subject-matter experts in electronic (and occasionally face-to-face) communities of practice. ConocoPhillips's Networks of Excellence is an example of this kind of community of practice—albeit with a slightly different name (chapter 7). Regardless of the terms used, what these groups have in common is interest in a particular (most often technical) knowledge domain and a practice of helping members solve problems in that domain. The electronic knowledge exchanges can function asynchronously and across the globe. The sidebar "Alcoa's Centers of Excellence and Ma'aden Aluminum in Saudi Arabia"

# Alcoa's Centers of Excellence and Ma'aden Aluminum in Saudi Arabia

Alcoa has several centers of excellence, the oldest of which focuses on smelting. Every business unit has its own center of excellence (CoE), composed of highly experienced specialists. The CoEs not only support plants with problem solving and "firefighting," but also have identified, codified, and diffused numerous key best practices benchmarked in their own and competitors' operations. These best practices must pass multiple stages of scrutiny by the relevant experts before being sanctioned and deployed. The practices are extensively documented and used to monitor and assess plant performance and to serve as the basis for continuous improvement. To be certified, a plant must achieve and maintain an average grade of 85 percent compliance to the best-practice requirements.

The resulting highly developed repositories of process knowledge have proven very useful in Alcoa's $10.8 billion joint venture with Ma'aden in Saudi Arabia—which is the lowest-cost aluminum production operation in the world. CoE smelting experts work closely with their Saudi counterparts to monitor operations at the Ras Al Khair smelter, providing Alcoa's expertise and experience. For example, in the delicate operation of bringing the smelting pots online, key processes must be precisely executed and parameters followed to ensure successful start-up. The CoE's experts provide guidance to plant personnel to achieve this start-up within operating, technical, and environmental control parameters. Because all the pots can be monitored in real time either remotely or on-site, personnel can quickly adjust parameters as needed.

The CoE has also provided on-site experts to the joint venture for assignments lasting from a few weeks to five years. The potroom start-up manager, for example, hails from Deschambault, Canada, which is the center's home base and where he gained the expertise that he is sharing with his Saudi counterpart. Because of the continuous nature of the smelting production process, it is essential that the Saudi pot-room manager master the process and understand key indicators so as to stay on top of things and anticipate problems before they occur. The lessons the experts impart are both technical and about day-to-day management, including the importance of walking the shop floor to stay connected to actual operations and to resolve process deviations.[a]

a. Mike Barriere, Roberto Andrade, Jim Lundy, Natalie Schilling, and Greg Bashore, telephone interviews with the authors, August 1, 2013, and September 5, 2013.

describes how Alcoa has utilized its centers of excellence to transfer essential knowledge to its joint venture in Saudi Arabia.

But if your organization does not have such an electronic network set up, how can you address the issue of a geographic distance between your experts and learners?

Today, it is a rare organization that does not face geographic dispersion. But fortunately, we also have media that are "richer" than ever. Video conferencing and other technologies allow a lot of personal—and visual—interaction. Some of the techniques suggested in the book are obviously amenable to long-distance application. Smart questioning over the telephone can be very effective. Even OPPTY can be done remotely. While this process is certainly most beneficial when the expert and learner are colocated, OPPTY is currently being used in organizations when the two are separated by thousands of miles—and even by native language. The mini-experiences so essential to this tool have to be creatively devised, but, for example, an engineer in Germany can visit a client in his or her own country and can be both coached on what to observe and also debriefed about the experience after the fact, by the expert in the United States.

## Limitations of Recipients

Are new hires an obstacle or an opportunity? Well, both! The final major obstacle identified by our survey recipients may reflect an inability or unwillingness of some younger workers to learn from their elders. Twenty percent of our respondents gave as their number one or number two obstacle to knowledge transfer either "new hires lack basic foundational knowledge to absorb expertise," or "younger employees are uninterested in learning from experts." The first of these, as discussed in chapter 3, refers to the knowledge gap between learner and expert—a gap that can be bridged only when the learner develops that foundational knowledge. It is up to both the expert and the learner to identify what the learner can do to develop the necessary receptors and basic knowledge—or perhaps to decide that the original matching of expert and learner was unwise because the gap is too wide. But in the OPPTY process, if there is a knowledge-sharing coach such as described in the GEGRC example, the coach can facilitate the decision about how to close the gap.

If the issue is more motivational and reflects either the high self-confidence of some smart millennials or a fundamental misunderstanding or even lack of appreciation on their part for the importance of hard-won experience, then there are other solutions. When you envision a mentor working with a mentee, you likely envision a graybeard dispensing pearls of wisdom to a young acolyte. But that vision probably won't resonate with a typical Gen-Y or millennial worker. These young people, born in the last quarter of the twentieth century, bring a mind-set that is quite different from their Gen-X and baby boomer predecessors. And there are a lot of this youngest cohort of workers! As of 2010, there were 88 million millennials in the United States, compared with 50 million Gen-Xers.[10] So while not all knowledge-transfer efforts are directed at millennials, this age group is increasingly filling the managerial ranks. Many of the high-level executives we interviewed reported that millennials often had little loyalty to the company, were impatient to advance through the ranks, wanted flexible schedules, and preferred communicating through social media. As HR executive George Rosato of Consol Energy notes, "my involvement with new hires shows that they will research the answer digitally before questioning or seeking advice from the experienced employees. This may give the perception that the digital natives feel so empowered by their access to information on the web that they see little value in learning from the past."[11] Such perceptions can be unsettling to older executives whose careers have been shaped by hands-on experience aided by one or more trusted mentors.

So what can managers do to address this potential obstacle? Companies are taking one or both of two strategies: (1) teach and socialize; and (2) recognize and utilize. Let's look at a few examples.

## Teach and Socialize

Executives like Rosato are giving a lot of thought to how they can inspire organizational loyalty in the millennials and how they can best use the skills of this young group. Consol Energy offers a tuition program for formal education leading to a college or graduate degree. The company's IT organization also has a budget for specialized training in a given skill or computer language. And, perhaps most attractive to millennials, Consol's IT organization offers a more flexible work schedule, allowing the employee to choose start and end times, provided that core hour coverage is supplied within their specialty area.

At Cisco Systems, job responsibilities are clear, and Cisco has identified job competencies from beginner to advanced. Cisco helps new hires achieve these competencies through a learning plan tied to completion of courses. However, the newbies also need to understand less obvious requirements for promotion. Successful Cisco employees generally make lateral moves, to gain experience in adjacent functions such as marketing or HR and through transfers to Cisco's far-flung centers abroad. This careful and traditional plan for advancement can conflict with millennials' expectations, including those for rapid advancement (see the sidebar "Millennial Challenges for Cisco in India"). Cisco and its managers have addressed unrealistic expectations in two ways. First, they have created rich stories, with visual maps and videos, based on employees who have had spectacular careers with the company, including the requisite lateral moves around the world. Such stories illustrate the rich experience that successful executives have accrued. And second, Cisco is building programs around job rotation, working to convince people that when they rotate to a position overseas, they will still have a job when they return.[12]

## Recognize and Utilize Millennial Skills

Millennials may also bring to their companies important skills and ways of solving problems. While they are impatient to advance, they

# Millennial Challenges for Cisco in India

Of course, the challenges of transferring knowledge to millennials are not peculiar to organizations in America. In Bangalore, India, 85 percent of Cisco's employees are twenty-nine or younger. Management must work with people whose expectations include a promotion every year. According to Barry Shields, head of business architecture for learning and development at Cisco, "They don't know what they don't know. They don't know about the roles across Cisco, that for example, a person can go from being a manager back to being an individual contributor. They don't truly understand what it takes to get promoted—a breadth of experience within the technology industry, for example, is a good starting point. They have a linear view of a career and they expect that if they earn their salary and learn quickly, they will get a grade level bump every year, which is not necessarily the case. Also, they feel that if they aren't going up, they are not succeeding—and are likely to leave."[a]

a. Barry Shields, interview with the authors, July 28, 2013.

are eager to learn and seek assistance wherever they can find it. They want answers quickly and have a large menu of electronic tools they can tap to get those answers. A significant number of companies are experimenting with *reverse mentoring*, that is, having younger experts tutor their seniors. For example, Jeanne Meister and Karie Willyerd propose reverse mentoring as a way for millennials both to gain access to—and to learn from—more senior executives and to enrich the organization by transferring their skills in crowdsourcing, open innovation, and social media.[13] For example, how can customers be reached more quickly and efficiently, or new markets be better tapped through a deeper knowledge of social media? Both generations gain—for the millennials, "a potentially accelerated career track, as the mentoring arrangement raises their profile among senior executives of the firm."[14] And the mentees learn the skills that may be necessary in the post-digital age. Newer hires may also bring new perspectives to a familiar task.

In the Technology and Innovation Center of Excellence at Alcoa, President Roberto Andrade has an almost fifty-fifty mix of very senior engineers and very young ones. Not all the knowledge flows one way. For example, a recent hire with a PhD in statistics successfully and beneficially challenged a longtime practice. The performance of a plant's furnaces used to be based on an average of all the furnaces. The new hire demonstrated that Alcoa was better served by observing each furnace and responding to individual variances in furnace performance. The application of statistics to a decade of data collected by Alcoa's "Smart" recording system has resulted in large savings—enough gains to equal adding an additional $2–3 million to the typical improvement in yield that Alcoa routinely achieves through process improvement.[15]

# Knowledge Sharing All the Time, Everywhere

Knowledge sharing is a part of every job, every day. Intellectually, we know this. But urgency has a tendency to drive out importance. We are all busier than seems humanly feasible. Unless we build knowledge sharing into an expected prerequisite for every promotion, every rotation, every retirement, we will fall short of ideal. And we can recognize people who share their knowledge freely. We can't change everything all at once. But we hope we can all move toward that goal.

The more that knowledge sharing can be built into onboarding, succession planning, retirement planning, and routine rotations, the more that we will avoid the costs described in chapter 1 and overcome the obstacles enumerated in this final chapter.

Our objectives in writing this book include providing you with some tools, to be sure. We hope you will find some that help you avoid unnecessary costs during job transitions or help you absorb the smarts you need to progress in your career. But we are a bit more ambitious. We hope we have also alerted you to the need to explore the wonderful, complex, often unappreciated realm of experience that grows within *every* individual's mind—to value it and nourish it. Tacit knowledge need not be invisible. Deep smarts need not be lost.

# Notes

## Introduction

1. Joshua Brustein, "Fix This," *Bloomberg Businessweek*, March 10–16, 2014, 68.

## Chapter 1

1. Mark Peters and David Wessel, "What's Wrong in Fort Wayne?" *Wall Street Journal*, December 7, 2012, B1, B4.

2. Jim Bethmann, interview with the authors, July 8 and 26, 2013. A specific example is when game company Zynga replaced its founder CEO in July 2013 with an outsider from Microsoft. As reported in Douglas MacMillan, "Zynga Is Said to Lose Three Top Executives After CEO Change" (*Bloomberg Businessweek*, July 30, 2013), three top executives fled, including Zynga's vice president of all games and its senior vice president of games, both of whom had guided the groups responsible for Zynga's popular games such as CityVille and FarmVille. This departure followed a previous exodus by a number of employees who have used their talents to create at least six direct competitors to Zynga. The costs of losing such talent are stratospheric; the incoming CEO must dig out of a deep hole.

3. John T. Edge, "How the Microplane Grater Escaped the Garage," *New York Times*, January 11, 2011, D1.

4. John Tracy, telephone interview with authors (DL and WS), June 6, 2013.

## Chapter 2

1. Thomas Davenport and Laurence Prusak, *Working Knowledge: How Organizations Manage What They Know* (Boston: Harvard Business School Press, 1998), 3.

2. Dorothy Leonard and Sylvia Sensiper, "The Role of Tacit Knowledge in Group Innovation," *California Management Review* 40, no. 3 (1998): 113.

3. David Eagleman, "The Mystery of Expertise," *The Week*, December 30, 2011–January 6, 2012, 48–49.

4. Christopher Seaman, "What Is That Conductor Up To?" *Wall Street Journal*, August 3–4, 2013, C3.

5. Steven Pinker, "The Mystery of Consciousness," *Time*, January 29, 2007, 60–61.

6. John W. Miller, "Mining Firms Discover Old-Timers Can Be Worth Their Weight in Gold," *Wall Street Journal*, March 4, 2013, A12.

7. Buzz Williams, interview with author (DL) and David Thomas, October 10, 2006.

8. Lisa Sanders, "A Wound That Won't Heal," *New York Times Magazine*, November 11, 2012, 22, 24.

9. Howard Schneiderman, dean of Biological Sciences at the University of California, Irvine, quoted in Dorothy Leonard-Barton and Gary Pisano, *Monsanto's March into Biotechnology*, Case 9-690-009 (Boston: Harvard Business School, 1992), 3.

10. Katie Hafner, "Could a Computer Outthink This Doctor?" *New York Times*, December 4, 2012, D1 and D6.

11. Ibid.

12. Dan Patrick, "Just My Type," interview with Steve Nash, *Sports Illustrated*, April 9, 2012, 22.

13. Mark Peters and David Wessel, "What's Wrong in Fort Wayne?" *Wall Street Journal*, December 7, 2012, B1, B4.

14. K. Anders Ericsson, Michael J. Prietula, and Edward T. Cokely, "The Making of an Expert," *Harvard Business Review*, July–August 2007, 114–121.

15. Gary Klein, *The Power of Intuition* (New York: Doubleday, 2003), 5–6.

16. Daniel Kahneman, *Thinking, Fast and Slow* (New York: Farrar, Straus and Giroux, 2011), 240.

17. Julie Cart, "Mapping Fires: Unpredictability Is the New Normal," *Los Angeles Times*, July 6, 2013.

18. Nassim Taleb, "Learning to Love Volatility," *Wall Street Journal*, November 17–18, 2012, C2.

## Chapter 3

1. Lauren Weber, "Rehire a Retiree? Maybe Not," *At Work (Wall Street Journal* blog), April 3, 2013.

2. Wesley Vestal, "RELAY Structured Mentoring/Knowledge Transfer Process," paper presented at the annual APQC KM Conference, Chicago, April 28–May 2, 2008.

3. Gary Ballinger, Elizabeth Craig, Rob Cross, and Peter Gray, "A Stitch in Time Saves Nine: Leveraging Networks to Reduce the Costs of Turnover," *California Management Review* 53, no. 4 (Summer 2010): 10–11.

4. Carlota Vollhardt, "Pfizer's Prescription for the Risky Business of Executive Transitions," *Journal of Organizational Excellence* (Winter 2005).

## Chapter 4

1. See http://www.ideaconnection.com.

2. Wesley Vestal, HR director for Baker Hughes Integrated Operations, email to author (DL), November 17, 2013.

3. Holly C. Baxter, "Trends and Best Practices for Improving Knowledge Transfer Across the Globe," paper presented at the Interservice/Industry Training, Simulation, and Education Conference (I/ITSEC), 2011.

4. Dan Ranta, director of knowledge sharing, ConocoPhillips, interview with authors, October 10, 2013.

## Chapter 5

1. Walter Swap et al., "Using Mentoring and Storytelling to Transfer Knowledge in the Workplace," *Journal of Management Information Systems* 18, no. 1 (Summer 2001): 95–114.

2. Much of this description is taken from Robert Sullivan, "Heroes of the Underground," *New York Times*, October 27, 2013, 34–40.

3. Jim Bethmann, interview with the authors, July 8, 2013.

4. Kent Greenes, email to author (DL), November 11, 2013.

5. Katrina B. Pugh, *Sharing Hidden Know-How: How Managers Solve Thorny Problems with the Knowledge Jam* (San Francisco: Jossey-Bass, 2011).

6. James Steele, interview with author (DL) and David Thomas, August 2, 2006.

## Chapter 6

1. Pamela M. Auble, Jeffrey J. Franks, and Salvatore A. Soraci, "Effort Toward Comprehension: Elaboration or 'Aha'?" *Memory and Cognition* 7 (1978): 426–434.

2. Lt. Col. Tony Burgess, email to author (DL), November 10, 2013.

3. Chris Miller, Nate Self, and Sena Garven, "Leader Challenge: A Platform for Training and Developing Leaders," paper presented at the Interservice/Industry Training, Simulation, and Education Conference (I/ITSEC), 2009.

4. Holly C. Baxter et al., "Leveraging Commercial Video Game Technology to Improve Military Decision Skills," Interservice/Industry Training, Simulation and Training Conference (I/ITSEC), 2004.

5. Holly C. Baxter, "Transferring Specialized Knowledge: Accelerating the Expertise Development Cycle," paper 13193, paper presented at the Interservice/Industry Training, Simulation, and Education Conference, 2013, 7.

6. Ashlee Vance, "Ansys Is Out to Simulate the World," *Bloomberg Businessweek*, March 11–March 17, 2013, 32–34.

## Chapter 7

1. Dan Ranta, "ConocoPhillips 2012 MAKE Finalist Case Study," corporate publication, 2012, 10 (used with permission).

2. Rob Cross et al., eds., *The Organizational Network Fieldbook: Best Practices, Techniques, and Exercises to Drive Organizational Innovation and Performance* (San Francisco: Jossey-Bass, 2010), 11–21.

3. Richard McDermott and Douglas Archibald, "Harnessing Your Staff's Informal Networks," *Harvard Business Review*, March 2010, 82–89.

4. Ranta, "ConocoPhillips 2012 MAKE Finalist."

5. Jeff Stemke, email to authors (DL), October 8, 2013.

6. Hubert L. Dreyfus and Stuart E. Dreyfus, *Mind over Machine* (New York: Free Press, 1986).

7. Jennifer K. Phillips, Karol G. Ross, and Scott B. Shadrick, "User's Guide for Tactical Thinking, Behaviorally Anchored Rating Scales," Armored Forces Research Unit, United States Army Research Institute for the Behavioral and Social Sciences, 2006.

8. Holly C. Baxter, email to author (DL), July 17, 2013.

## Chapter 8

1. Matt Sedensky, "More Are Phasing In Their Retirement with Part-Time Schedule," *Arizona Daily Star*, May 30, 2013, A13.

2. Dorothy Leonard and Steven Labate, "Rehiring Retirees as Consultants Is Bad Business!" *HBR Blog Network*, March 29, 2013.

3. Martin Dewhurst, Bryan Hancock, and Diana Ellsworth, "Redesigning Knowledge Work," *Harvard Business Review*, January–February 2013, 58–64.

## Chapter 9

1. Manuel Becerra, Randi Lunnan, and Lars Huemer, "Trustworthiness, Risk, and the Transfer of Tacit and Explicit Knowledge Between Alliance Partners," *Journal of Management Studies* 45, no. 4 (2008): 691–713.

2. Teresa Amabile and Steven Kramer, *The Progress Principle: Using Small Wins to Ignite Joy, Engagement, and Creativity at Work* (Boston: Harvard Business Review Press, 2011), 71.

3. Splish Splash, comment on Dorothy Leonard and Steven Labate, "Rehiring Retirees as Consultants Is Bad Business!" *HBR Blog Network*, March 29, 2013, http://blogs.hbr.org/2013/03/stop-paying-your-experts-to-ho/.

4. Teresa M. Amabile, *Creativity in Context* (Boulder, CO: Westview, 1996).

5. Kent Greenes, email to author (DL), November 11, 2013.

6. Dorothy Leonard and Walter Swap, *When Sparks Fly: Igniting Creativity in Groups* (Boston: Harvard Business School Publishing, 1999), 186.

7. Hassan Rmaile, telephone interview with the authors (DL, WS), June 3, 2013.

8. Kiho Sohn, telephone interview with the authors (DL, WS), June 10, 2013.

9. Susan Rosenbaum, email to author (DL), October 15, 2013.

10. Jeanne C. Meister and Karie Willyerd, "Mentoring Millennials," *Harvard Business Review*, May 2010, 69.

11. George Rosato, telephone interview with the authors (DL, WS), August 2, 2013.

12. Barry Shields, telephone interview with the authors (DL, WS), June 27, 2013.

13. Meister and Willyerd, "Mentoring Millennials."

14. Ibid., 70.

15. Roberto Andrade, interview with the authors (DL, WS), September 5, 2013.

# References

Amabile, Teresa M. *Creativity in Context*. Boulder, CO: Westview, 1996.

Amabile, Teresa, and Steven Kramer. *The Progress Principle: Using Small Wins to Ignite Joy, Engagement, and Creativity at Work*. Boston: Harvard Business Review Press, 2011.

Ambady, Nalini, Mary Anne Krabbenhoft, and Daniel Hogan. "30-Sec Sale: Using Thin-Slice Judgments to Evaluate Sales Effectiveness." *Journal of Consumer Psychology* 16, no. 1 (2006): 4–13.

Auble, Pamela M., Jeffrey J. Franks, and Salvatore A. Soraci. "Effort Toward Comprehension: Elaboration or 'Aha'?" *Memory and Cognition* 7 (1978): 426–434.

Ballinger, Gary, Elizabeth Craig, Rob Cross, and Peter Gray. "A Stitch in Time Saves Nine: Leveraging Networks to Reduce the Costs of Turnover." *California Management Review* 53, no. 4 (Summer 2010): 1–23.

Baum, Dan. "Battle Lessons: What the Generals Don't Know." *New Yorker*, January 17, 2005, 42–48.

Baxter, Holly C. "Transferring Specialized Knowledge: Accelerating the Expertise Development Cycle." Paper 13193. Paper presented at the Interservice/Industry Training, Simulation, and Education Conference, 2013, 1–9.

Baxter, Holly C., Karol G. Ross, Jennifer Phillips, Jennifer Shafer, and Jennifer Fowlkes. "Leveraging Commercial Video Game Technology to Improve Military Decision Skills." Interservice/Industry Training, Simulation and Training Conference (I/ITSEC), 2004.

Baxter, Holly C. "Trends and Best Practices for Improving Knowledge Transfer Across the Globe." Paper presented at the Interservice/Industry Training, Simulation, and Education Conference (I/ITSEC), 2011.

Becerra, Manuel, Randi Lunnan, and Lars Huemer. "Trustworthiness, Risk, and the Transfer of Tacit and Explicit Knowledge Between Alliance Partners." *Journal of Management Studies* 45, no. 4 (2008): 691–713.

Brustein, Joshua. "Fix This." *Bloomberg Businessweek*, March 10–16, 2014, 68.

Carey, Benedict. "Come On, I Thought I Knew That!" *New York Times*, April 19, 2011, D5–D6.

Cart, Julie. "Mapping Fires: Unpredictability Is the New Normal." *Los Angeles Times*, July 6, 2013.

Cross, Rob, Jean Singer, Sally Colella, Robert J. Thomas, and Yaarit Silverstone, eds. *The Organizational Network Fieldbook: Best Practices, Techniques, and Exercises to Drive Organizational Innovation and Performance*. San Francisco: Jossey-Bass, 2010.

Davenport, Thomas, and Laurence Prusak. *Working Knowledge: How Organizations Manage What They Know*. Boston: Harvard Business School Press, 1998.

Dewhurst, Martin, Bryan Hancock, and Diana Ellsworth. "Redesigning Knowledge Work." *Harvard Business Review*, January–February 2013, 58–64.

Dreyfus, Hubert L., and Stuart E. Dreyfus. *Mind over Machine*. New York: Free Press, 1986.

Eagleman, David. "The Mystery of Expertise." *The Week*, December 30, 2011–January 6, 2012, 48–49.

Edge, John T. "How the Microplane Grater Escaped the Garage." *New York Times*, January 11, 2011, D1.

Ericsson, K. Anders, Michael J. Prietula, and Edward T. Cokely. "The Making of an Expert." *Harvard Business Review*, July–August 2007, 114–121.

Hafner, Katie. "Could a Computer Outthink This Doctor?" *New York Times*, December 4, 2012, D1 and D6.

Kahneman, Daniel. *Thinking, Fast and Slow*. New York: Farrar, Straus and Giroux, 2011.

Klein, Gary. *The Power of Intuition*. New York: Doubleday, 2003.

Lehrer, Jonah. "Groupthink: The Brainstorming Myth." *New Yorker*, January 30, 2012, www.newyorker.com/reporting/2012/01/30/120130fa_fact_lehrer.

Leonard-Barton, Dorothy, and Gary Pisano. *Monsanto's March into Biotechnology*. Case 9-690-009. Boston: Harvard Business School, 1992.

Leonard, Dorothy, and Sylvia Sensiper. "The Role of Tacit Knowledge in Group Innovation." *California Management Review* 40, no. 3 (Spring 1998).

Leonard, Dorothy, and Walter Swap. *Deep Smarts: How to Cultivate and Transfer Enduring Business Wisdom*. Boston: Harvard Business School Publishing, 2005.

———. *When Sparks Fly: Igniting Creativity in Groups*. Boston: Harvard Business School Publishing, 1999.

Leonard, Dorothy, and Steven Labate. "Rehiring Retirees as Consultants Is Bad Business!" *HBR Blog Network*, March 29, 2013.

Leonard, Dorothy, and Tim Bridges. "Why Kids—and Workers—Need to Get Their Hands Dirty." *HBR Blog Network*, October 9, 2013. http://blogs.hbr.org/2013/10/why-kids-and-workers-need-to-get-their-hands-dirty/.

MacMillan, Douglas. "Zynga Is Said to Lose Three Top Executives After CEO Change." *Bloomberg Businessweek*, July 30, 2013.

McDermott, Richard, and Douglas Archibald. "Harnessing Your Staff's Informal Networks." *Harvard Business Review*, March 2010, 82–89.

Meister, Jeanne C., and Karie Willyerd. "Mentoring Millennials." *Harvard Business Review*, May 2010, 68–72.

Miller, Chris, Nate Self, and Sena Garven. "Leader Challenge: A Platform for Training and Developing Leaders." Paper presented at the Interservice/Industry Training, Simulation, and Education Conference (I/ITSEC), 2009.

Miller, John W. "Mining Firms Discover Old-Timers Can Be Worth Their Weight in Gold." *Wall Street Journal*, March 4, 2013, A1 and A12.

Neil, Dan. "The Driverless Road Ahead." *Wall Street Journal*, September 28–29, 2013, D1–D2.

Newcomb, Tim. "Fast-Tracking: GPS Use Is on the Rise in the NFL." *Sports Illustrated*, November 4, 2013, 20.

Parise, Salvatore, Rob Cross, and Thomas H. Davenport. "Strategies for Preventing a Knowledge-Loss Crisis." *MIT Sloan Management Review* 47, no. 4 (Summer 2006): 31–38.

Pasztor, Andy, Yoree Koh, and Yoshio Takahashi. "Needed: Battery Expertise for Probe." *Wall Street Journal*, February 27, 2013, B8.

Patrick, Dan. "Just My Type." Interview with Steve Nash. *Sports Illustrated*, April 9, 2012, 22.

Peters, Mark, and David Wessel. "What's Wrong in Fort Wayne?" *Wall Street Journal*, December 7, 2012, B1, B4.

Phillips, Jennifer K., Karol G. Ross, and Scott B. Shadrick. "User's Guide for Tactical Thinking, Behaviorally Anchored Rating Scales." Armored Forces Research Unit, United States Army Research Institute for the Behavioral and Social Sciences, 2006.

Pinker, Steven. "The Mystery of Consciousness." *Time*, January 29, 2007, 60–61.

Pugh, Katrina B. *Sharing Hidden Know-How: How Managers Solve Thorny Problems with the Knowledge Jam.* San Francisco: Jossey-Bass, 2011.

Ranta, Dan. "ConocoPhillips 2012 MAKE Finalist Case Study." Corporate publication, 2012, 10. Used with permission.

Reuell, Peter. "Understanding Student Weaknesses." *Harvard Gazette*, April 30, 2013, http://news.harvard.edu/gazette/story/2013/04/understanding-student-weaknesses.

Sanders, Lisa. "A Wound That Won't Heal." *New York Times Magazine*, November 11, 2012, 22, 24.

Schlumberger Business Consulting website, 2012, www.sbc.slb.com.

Seaman, Christopher. "What Is That Conductor Up To?" *Wall Street Journal*, August 3–4, 2013, C3.

Sedensky, Matt. "More Are Phasing In Their Retirement with Part-Time Schedule." *Arizona Daily Star*, May 30, 2013, A13.

Stone, Alex. *Fooling Houdini: Magicians, Mentalists, Math Geeks, and the Hidden Powers of the Mind.* Chapter 4, "The Touch Analyst." New York: HarperCollins, 2012.

Sullivan, Robert. "Heroes of the Underground." *New York Times*, October 27, 2013, 34–40.

Sutherland, Jeff. *Scrum: The Art of Doing Twice the Work in Half the Time.* New York: Crown Business, 2014.

Swap, Walter, Dorothy Leonard, Mimi Shields, and Lisa Abrams. "Using Mentoring and Storytelling to Transfer Knowledge in the Workplace." *Journal of Management Information Systems* 18, no. 1 (Summer 2001): 95–114.

Taleb, Nassim. "Learning to Love Volatility." *Wall Street Journal*, November 17–18, 2012, C1–C2.

Unger, Jason. "Can Monkeys Pick Stocks Better than Experts?" *Automatic Finances.* Accessed May 20, 2014. www.automaticfinances.com/monkey-stock-picking/.

Vance, Ashlee. "Ansys Is Out to Simulate the World." *Bloomberg Businessweek*, March 11–March 17, 2013, 32–34.

———. "Ramona Pierson Got Run Over, Went into a Coma, Woke Up Blind, and Is Launching One of the Most Original Tech Companies in Years." *Bloomberg Businessweek*, September 30–October 6, 2013, 86–90.

Vestal, Wesley. "RELAY Structured Mentoring/Knowledge Transfer Process." Paper presented at the annual APQC KM Conference, Chicago, April 28–May 2, 2008.

Vollhardt, Carlota. "Pfizer's Prescription for the Risky Business of Executive Transitions." *Journal of Organizational Excellence* (Winter 2005).

Weber, Lauren. "Rehire a Retiree? Maybe Not." *At Work* (*Wall Street Journal* blog), April 3, 2013.

# Index

*Note:* page numbers followed by *f* indicate figures; page numbers followed by *t* indicate tables; page numbers followed by *n* indicate endnotes.

Agilent Technologies, 75
Alcoa, 133, 193–194, 199
Allen, Nate, 76–77
Amabile, Teresa, 185
Andrade, Robert, 194, 199
Ansys, 140

Baker Hughes, 47–48, 78–79, 121, 166
Bank of America, 57, 58–60
Barriere, Mike, 194*n*
Bashore, Greg, 194*n*
Baxter, Holly, 79, 139, 154
best practices, 86, 90–91, 103, 108,
    113, 146, 148–149, 169, 173,
    193–194
Bethmann, Jim, 11,101–102
big data, 3
black swans, 41
Boeing, 14–15, 35–36, 164
Bonito, Joe, 60*n*
Bridges, Tim, 35–36
British Petroleum, 83
BroadScopes, 70–74
Burgess, Tony, 76–77

Caldwell Partners, 101–102
Capossela, Chris, 129
Cashman, Jim, III, 140
Cav.net, 77
centers of excellence at Alcoa,
    193–194, 199

Chevron, 148–149
Cisco Systems, 197–198
coach, coaching, 37, 45, 55, 57–59,
    120–121, 170–171, 173–174, 178,
    188, 196
communities of practice, 60, 74,
    76–78, 147, 191, 193. *See also*
    Networks of Excellence, centers
    of excellence
Companycommand.com, 77
confirmation bias, 105
ConocoPhillips, 85, 147–148, 193
Consol Energy, 196–197
critical incident
    analysis of, 92–98
    as simulation, 141
    facilitation about, 95–96
    Hurricane Sandy, 97–98
    protocol, 96
    selection of, 92–94
Cuomo, Andrew, 97

Declara, 49
deep smarts
    characteristics and indicators of,
        25–38, 104–110, 157*t*, 158,
        159*t*, 160
    communication, 31–32, 157*t*,
        159*t*
    context awareness, 28–29, 104,
        108, 157*t*, 159*t*
    critical skills, 51, 104, 157*t*

deep smarts (*continued*)
    diagnosis, 32–33, 104, 109, 112
    interpersonal skills, 31, 105, 157
    judgment, 28–29, 51
    networking, 30–31, 157*t*, 159*t*
    pattern recognition, 29–30, 119,
        141, 157*t*
    personality-based skills, 37, 105
    rapid, wise decision making, 157*t*
    sensory intelligence, 33–36, 105,
        109
    system perspective, 27–28, 51,
        104, 108, 119, 141, 157*t*
  definition, 2
  gap assessment tool, 156–161
  interviews, 104–110 (*see also*
    knowledge elicitation)
  research on, 39, 50–52, 107–108,
    110, 169
  self-presentation, bias in, 51,
    110–111
  self-report, 110
  targeting, 72–74, 179–180
  unnoticed, 43–45, 48–49
  validating, 110–112
deliberate practice, 38, 130
Dhaliwal, Gurpreet, 32

Ericsson, K. Anders, 37
exit interview, 78–80, 84
experience, 18, 73–74, 115, 118–121
  guided (*see* OPPTY)
  limits of, 39
  vicarious, 115, 118–119
expertise
  as know-how, 2–3
  attaining, 35–38
  coach's, 178
  examples of, 19, 37, 52, 113–114,
    122–124
  implicit dimensions of, 20–21
  learners' own, 53
  levels of, 150–151
  reluctance to share, 189–190
  survey about, 14
  *See also* experts
experts, 40, 105–112, 122–135, 170,
  180

  identification of, 46–52
    deep smarts survey approach, 50
    engineer's approach, 47–48
    organizational network analysis
      approach 48–49
    upper-management approach
      51–52
  versus monkeys, 40
  *See also* expertise

facilitation, 83–85, 91–92, 95–96
Fort Wayne Metals, 36

GE Global Research Centers (GEGRC)
  assessing risk of knowledge loss,
    166–168
  knowledge transfer program,
    163–178, 188, 190
    indicators of success, 176–177
    lessons learned, 177–178
    selecting a strategy, 168–170
    hiring retirees, 164–165, 190
Giulini, Carlo Maria, 23
Greenes, Kent, 83–84, 102–103,
  191–192

H. B. Fuller, 191

IBM's Watson for Healthcare, 33
*Idea Connection Innovation Newsletter*,
  78
information technology, 76–77. *See
  also* communities of practice
Institute for Healthcare
  Improvement, 103–104
intuition, 29, 39

Jezycki, Frank, 97

Kahneman, Daniel, 39
Klein, Gary, 39
K.L. Hagen and Associates, 80, 82,
  99, 182

knowledge elicitation, 57, 68–69, 74–75,
  79–84, 90–91, 95, 108, 154, 173
  deep smarts interviews, 104–110
  knowledge jams, 103–104
  peer assists, 102–103
  project histories, 98–100
  stories, 91–101
  See also smart questioning
knowledge gap, 53–55
knowledge transfer
  accelerating transfer of tacit
    knowledge, 119–135
  apprenticeship (see OPPTY)
  archiving, 84–85, 112–114
  coaches, 55, 57, 196 (see also
    knowledge-sharing coach)
  consultants, 66, 169–170
  contract, 57, 60–61
  contract, at GEGRC, 173–175
  discovery method, 135–141
  facilitators, 55, 57, 90–92
  lessons learned, 178–180
  mapping, 113–114 (see also
    BroadScopes)
  match to techniques, 66
  measuring success, 143–161
    competency models in
      Schlumberger, 150–153
    competency models in the US
      Army, 150–151
    cost avoidance, 147–148
    diffusing best practices, 148
    gap closure, 155–161
    individual or group competency-
      based, 146, 149–161
    input versus output, 145–146
    knowledge accrual by learners,
      149–155
    network capability-based, 146–149
    participant satisfaction, 154
    strategic necessity, 144
    success stories, 147–149
    time savings, 148–149
  motivation to share, 189–192
  at Nucor Steel, 183–185
  obstacles to and removal of, 185–198
    at Medco, 186
    experts reluctant to share, 189–190
    geographical dispersion, 193

  limitations of recipients, 195–197
  no time, 186–189
  planning for, 60–61
  stakeholders, 45
  and strategy selection at GEGRC,
    168–170
  urgency 67–68, 75–77
  workshop at GEGRC, 169–177
    agenda and objectives, 173
    preliminary work, 172
knowledge-sharing coach, 170–174
  recommended characteristics, 171
knowledge
  at risk of loss, 143–144, 166–168
    (see also knowledge loss)
  definition of, 18
  distinct from data and information,
    17–18
  explicit, 18–20, 25, 30, 67–68, 73,
    99, 108, 114, 118, 146, 149
  false, 56
  implicit, 18–21, 67–75, 91–92, 104,
    108, 114, 118, 119, 146, 149, 187
  levels of, 20–21
  know-how, 72–74
  know-what, 72–74
  know-what versus know-how, 3
  tacit, 19–20, 21–25, 54, 68, 73–74,
    112, 114–115, 119–135, 149
    examples of, 21–23, 25, 54, 133,
      144
    levels of, 22–23
    re-creating, 119–120
    transfer of (see OPPTY)
    unconscious, 23
    visual cues, 23–25
  tactile, 34–35
knowledge loss
  costs of, 9–16, 144
    intangible costs, 12–13
    loss of innovation capacity, 13–15
    loss of productivity, 10–12
Kramer, Steven, 185

Labate, Steven, 165–171
learners, 52–53, 132, 134–135, 170
  as experts, 53
  as near experts, 170

learners (*continued*)
  receptors of, 53–55
  *See also* OPPTY
learning, 119–120, 127, 129, 135–137,
  176
  discovery method, 138–139
  trial and error, 66
learning log, 126, 129–134, 153,
  156, 173
Leonard-Barton Group, 80, 169,
  172, 178
Lundy, Jim, 194*n*

Ma'aden Aluminum, 193–194
Malkiel, Burton, 40
McLean, Scott, 25
Medco, 186
Meister, Jeanne, 198
mentor, mentoring, 36–38, 120–121,
  130, 144, 146, 152, 169, 173–174,
  188–192
  reverse, 198–199
  *See also* OPPTY
Microsoft, 129
Millennials, 1, 196–199
Miller, Katharine, 184*n*
Monette, Brian, 71

Nash, Steve, 33
Networks of Excellence (at
  ConocoPhillips), 147, 193
Nucor Steel, 183–185

O'Hara, Tim, 172, 176–177
onboarding, 58–60, 101–102
  at Bank of America, 58–60
OPPTY, 120–135, 156, 158, 160, 167,
  175–177, 195
  action plan, 123–126
  learning log, 126, 128–133, 155
  observation, 127–129
  partnering, 132–133
  practice, 130–131
  taking responsibility, 133
organizational culture, 1, 27, 75, 117,
  182–185, 190
  at Agilent, 75

at Baker Hughes, 121
at Nucor Steel, 183–185

pattern recognition, 3, 25–26, 29–30,
  32–33, 37, 39, 41, 105, 109, 119,
  157
peer assists. *See* knowledge elicitation
Perry, Phil, 47
Pfizer, 57, 60
Pierson, Ramona, 49
Pinker, Steven, 23
plane spotters, 22–23
Platoonleader.org, 77
practice, 33–34, 37–39, 68, 118,
  120–121, 124–125, 130–131,
  133, 173, 174–175, 177. *See also*
  deliberate practice
Prendergast, Thomas, 97
project histories. *See* knowledge
  elicitation
Pugh, Katrina, 103–104

quality function deployment (QFD) at
  GEGRC, 166

receptors, 53–55, 91, 119, 126, 153
  wrong, 55–56
Rmaile, Hassan, 191–192
Rosato, George, 196–197
Rousseau, Meta, 47

Schilling, Natalie, 194*n*
Schlumberger Business Consulting,
  150–153, 177, 192, 195
Schwartz, Jeremy, 29–30
Shields, Barry, 198
simulation, 3, 136, 139–141
smart questioning
  deep smarts interviews, 106
  question kits, 80–83
  templates, 80, 82–84
  what to ask, 74–75, 93–94, 96, 100,
    111, 128, 131–132
  who asks, 74
  *See also* knowledge elicitation
Sohn, Kiho, 192

Stanojevic, Nadine, 29–30
Steele, James, 107–108
Stemke, Jeff, 148–149
Stone, Alex, 34
Strategic Knowledge Solutions, 79, 154
survey of top executives, 12–14, 45, 135, 164, 185–189, 191–199

Taleb, Nassim, 41
thin-slice research, 23–24
Tracy, John, 15
Transition-Path, 70–72
Transitions Metals Corp., 25
Turner, Richard, 34

US Army, 76–77
   After Action Review, 83–84

Leader Challenge, 138–140
   levels of expertise in, 149–151
US Forest Service, 107

Vestal, Wesley, 47, 121n

*Wall Street Journal's* Dartboard
   Contest, 40
Wall, Josh, 184n
Willyerd, Karie, 198

Xerox, 188–189

Zen-Nippon Chicken Sexing
   School, 22

# Acknowledgments

We owe a debt of gratitude to the Harvard Business School's Division of Research, which generously supports even emeriti faculty in the production of intellectual capital. We could not have conducted the workshop on tacit knowledge that was a precipitating event for this book, nor the survey of practitioners that supplied such valuable content, without the research division's funding. For that help and the faith that we would use their support wisely, we especially thank Paul Healy and Toni Wegner. And we could not have managed the mechanics of the survey without the help of the staff at the Senior Faculty Center, namely Paula Alexander, Luz Velazquez, and Jean Antoniazzi.

Dozens of managers took time from their hectic lives to respond to the survey, and a surprising number volunteered for follow-up interviews. We can't acknowledge them all by name due to space constraints and also because many wished to have their candid remarks remain anonymous. But their stories enrich the book and ground it in the reality of all the challenges their roles present. We found our conversations with them inspiring and enlightening and we thank them. You know who you are!

Our editor, Courtney Cashman, helped us resist the siren calls of extended academic observations that could have diluted our message. And Allison Peter shepherded the manuscript through multiple editorial processes.

We thank four anonymous reviewers for taking the time to read the first draft and for persuading us to condense some of our otherwise deathless prose for the sake of our readers. Without their suggestions the book would be much longer.

People often ask us how three authors who also enjoy a close family relationship could risk their mutual affection with a grueling writing project such as this. The answer? Approach with caution— but where great mutual respect exists, the creative abrasion we have written about in prior publications actually works in practice.

# About the Authors

**Dorothy Leonard** is the William J. Abernathy Professor of Business Administration emerita at Harvard Business School. She served on the Harvard faculty for twenty years and before that taught at the Sloan School of Management, Massachusetts Institute of Technology. Her teaching, research, and consulting for major corporations and governments have focused on innovation, new-product development, creativity, and knowledge transfer. She served on a number of advisory boards and boards of directors for large and small companies.

Her more than one hundred publications appear in academic and practitioner journals and in books about innovation, knowledge assets, and human resource management. In addition, Professor Leonard has researched and written dozens of field-based text, video, and multi-media cases used in business school classrooms around the globe. Her book *Wellsprings of Knowledge: Building and Sustaining the Sources of Innovation*, published by Harvard Business School Publishing in 1995 and 1998, was seminal in the field of knowledge management. She has written two prior books with Walter Swap. *When Sparks Fly: Igniting Creativity in Groups* was first published in 1999 and was awarded "Best Book on Creativity" by the European Association for Creativity and Innovation. The widely cited book *Deep Smarts: How to Cultivate and Transfer Enduring Business Wisdom* was published in 2005 and translated into a dozen languages. In 2011, a collection of Professor Leonard's work, *Managing Knowledge Assets, Creativity and Innovation*, was issued by

World Scientific. In 2013, she was appointed a Leonardo Laureate in Europe for her "thought leadership in Knowledge Management, Innovation and Creativity."

**Walter Swap** is Professor of Psychology emeritus and former Chair of the Psychology Department at Tufts University. He served as a professor in the Gordon Institute at Tufts, which offers a degree in engineering management to practicing engineers and scientists. Dr. Swap was Dean of the Colleges for nine years, responsible for all aspects of undergraduate academic life at Tufts. He earned his bachelor's degree at Harvard and his PhD in social psychology at the University of Michigan.

Dr. Swap's professional life has been divided among teaching, research, and administration. He has received two awards for teaching excellence. He was a founding member of the Tufts Center for Decision Making, introducing undergraduates to the complexities of choice and group dynamics, and conducted workshops for managers from a variety of industries. As dean, he developed centers and programs promoting excellence in teaching, advising, critical thinking, and interdisciplinary education.

In addition to the two previous books coauthored with Dorothy Leonard, Dr. Swap's other publications include *Group Decision Making* and numerous book chapters and articles in professional journals on topics including group dynamics, attitude change, personality theory, altruism, and aggression.

**Gavin Barton** has focused his research and consulting practice on helping individuals and teams develop expertise. He is Managing Director of the Leonard-Barton Group, a company specializing in the development and transfer of expertise. He is also the principal and founder of GB Performance Consulting, a company that delivers personalized performance enhancement programs and educational, practice-based workshops for individuals and groups. In addition to coaching individuals, Dr. Barton has designed and implemented programs to enhance performance for different types of groups. He has applied his research and experience with reflective, experiential learning by professionals to business situations, in particular, to programs of knowledge sharing between in-house experts and their successors. For such programs, Dr. Barton has developed self-help tools for learners and experts.

Since obtaining his doctorate at Boston University, Dr. Barton has been an adjunct professor at Lasell College, where he teaches psychology and sport psychology. He has also been a frequent guest lecturer at Tufts University.

His current writing involves developing expertise, experiential learning, and enhancing life skills. His most recent article, "Make Yourself an Expert," was published in *Harvard Business Review* in April 2013.